Desert Air

Full many a flower is born to blush unseen
And waste its sweetness on the desert air.

Desert Air

A Collection of the Poetry of Place:
of Arabia, Deserts and the Orient
of the Imagination

Selected by
BARNABY ROGERSON
&
ALEXANDER MONRO

ELAND • LONDON

This arrangement and introduction © Barnaby Rogerson
Biographical notes © Alexander Monro & Barnaby Rogerson

ISBN 978 1 906011 05 5

First published in December 2001 by Eland Publishing Ltd,
61 Exmouth Market, Clerkenwell, London EC1R 4QL
This second edition published in October 2007

Pages designed and typeset by Antony Gray,
set in 8.5 and 11pt Berkeley.
Cover image:
E. J. H. Vernet's 'Arabs Travelling in the Desert' (1843)
Reproduced by permission of the
Trustees of the Wallace Collection, London.
Printed in Spain by GraphyCems

Introduction

This is a collection of poems that delights in constructing a sensual Orient of the imagination. It is a landscape where sand dunes bear the impress of a lover, where camel caravans process through the night laden with bales of precious merchandise. It is a place of walled citadels and tented encampments where the sons of noble sheikhs labour in dignity as shepherds. It is a land ruled by honour and hospitality, where poets and warriors are esteemed. It delights in catalogues: pagan gods, oases, trade goods, lineages and heroic virtues – be they of a camel, a horse or the profile of the beloved.

This landscape endures no barriers of time. It is found in the Song of Solomon, in the seven golden odes of pre-Islamic Arabia, in pavement cafés in Paris and London, in desert shacks and the new luxury hotels on the Persian Gulf. Its physical frontiers stretch out with the farthest boundaries of the Caliphate, to criss-cross the ancient world from Multan to Poitiers and from Samarkand to Timbuktu. It is neither good nor bad, true nor false but exists in the hidden expectations of the traveller.

The poetry has been grouped into two sections, so that the more familiar English verse about the Orient can serve as an introduction to the less well-known indigenous Arabic poetry. We initially planned to arrange the poems in a caravan-like trail that stretched across the lands of Islam, but as many of the landscapes are imaginary or unplaceable we have ordered them by age of composition (or translation) rather than by geography.

It is an intriguing irony of the English verse that the most popular and beloved, such as Shelley's 'Ozymandias' and Coleridge's 'Kubla Khan' were produced without any direct knowledge of the lands of Islam. None of the verses of experienced travellers can break this poetic colonisation of the East by the dream world of English Romanticism – to which, like deified heroes, we have added Pushkin, Goethe and Baudelaire. The English preference for poetic fiction should be treated as an intriguing self-revelation rather than a cause of righteous indignation. Certainly the charge of 'Orientalism' is all too self-evident in many of the verses. This should not however discourage us from acknowledging their quixotic championship of the Muslim East. The bonds of affection between Christendom and Islam are not so strong that we can afford to lose any of the partisans of this friendship. We should also admire the great oral quality of so many of these verses. At some time or other I have recited all of them to captive audiences of fellow travellers, perched on sand dunes, beside a ruined medieval city wall or the tarmac of a desert road at dusk. The effect has been magical, unearthing long-hidden memories and desires, while the very intoxication of the romantic imagery can surprisingly act like a purge, clearing away false values – but with a loving smile.

The second half of the collection is a personal hoard of some of the real poetry written in the 'desert air' and translated into English. It is not representative of anything apart from my erratic reading and chance gifts from friends. It expresses no literary judgement other than that of innocent delight. It is fitting that the collection should end at the beginning, with one of the earliest of the many English versions of the seven golden odes of pre-Islamic Arabia, verses so precious that they were hung beside the three hundred and sixty pagan statues that filled the Kaaba, ancient Arabia's holy of holies. When the Prophet

Muhammad (peace be upon him) cleansed this ancient religious shrine, the idols were destroyed but the poems were preserved.

If we can continue to thrill to the sound of such opening lines as: 'In Xanadu did Kubla Khan a stately pleasure-dome decree,' and 'I met a traveller from an antique land who said: two vast and trunkless legs of stone,' we should also remember a warning from the Koran,

> As for the poets – they that follow them go astray. Do you not see that they wander distraught in every vale, and that they say things which they do not do?

BARNABY ROGERSON

Acknowledgements

Dozens of friends and fellow travellers have assisted me in building up this collection with suggestions, references and photocopies tucked into letters. This information bank was much assisted by many a scribbled note taken down in the midst of a launch party. Those that I can remember sufficiently clearly to wish to thank include Barry Cole, Alan Jenkins, Edward Barker, Marius Kociejowski, Matthew Sturgis, John Lucas, Robert Irwin, Philippa Scott, Linda Kelly, Andrew Wilson, Fiona Gilmour-Eaves, Anthony Thwaite, Mary Miers, Hector McDonnell, Ateş Orga, Mungo McCosh and Charlie Boxer. Stephen Fennell has very kindly offered his original translations of Goethe to adorn this second edition.

I was fortunate to grow up amongst reciters, albeit it from a very small oeuvre. But for a child jammed in the back seat of a car betwixt siblings and basset hounds, on seemingly interminable journeys to campsites, race-meetings or meals with cousins, the sound of my mother's enthusiastic version of Longfellow's *Hiawatha* or Coleridge's *The Ancient Mariner*, balanced by my father's delight in the mischievous comic verse of fellow English Catholics such as Belloc and Chesterton, was the beginning of a lifelong delight in the spoken word. It is hoped that this book will continue the important work of amusing travellers.

Contents

PART TWO

Poems from the East

❋

PART ONE

THE EAST OF THE IMAGINATION

The Hymn

in 'On the Morning of Christ's Nativity'

Peor and Baalim
Forsake their temples dim,
With that twice-batter'd god of Palestine
And mooned Ashtaroth
Heaven's Queen and mother both,
Now sits not girt with tapers holy shine;
The Lybic Hammon shrinks his horn:
In vain the Tyrian maids their wounded Thammuz mourn.

And sullen Moloch, fled,
Hath left in shadows dread
His burning idol all of blackest hue;
In vain with cymbals' ring
They call the grisly king,
In dismal dance about the furnace blue:
The brutish gods of Nile as fast,
Isis, and Orus, and the dog Anubis haste.

Nor is Osiris seen
In Memphian grove, or green,
Trampling the unshower'd grass with lowings loud:
Nor can he be at rest
Within his sacred chest;
Nought but profoundest Hell can be his shroud:
In vain with timbrell'd anthems dark
The sable-stoled sorcerers bear his worshipt ark.

He feels from Juda's land
The dreaded infant's hand;
The rays of Bethlehem blind his dusky eye;
Nor all the gods beside
Longer dare abide,
Nor Typhon huge ending in snaky twine:
Our Babe, to show his Godhead true,
Can in His swaddling bands control the damned crew.

JOHN MILTON

Born in 1608, John Milton was one of the Common-wealth's most fervent supporters as well as one of its most useful ones. Some of his pamphlets supported the regicide of Charles I and the liberty of the press whilst others attacked divorce and episcopacy. First conceived in 1641, Milton's *magnum opus* was *Paradise Lost*, an epic poem that he had initially envisaged as a play. It was published in 1667, seven years before his death.

Abou ben Adhem

Abou Ben Adhem (may his tribe increase!)
Awoke one night from a deep dream of peace,
And saw, within the moonlight in his room,
Making it rich, and like a lily in bloom,
An angel writing in a book of gold: –
Exceeding peace had made Ben Adhem bold,
And to the presence in the room he said,
'What writest thou?' – The vision raised its head,
And with a look made of all sweet accord,
Answered, 'The names of those who love the Lord.'
'And is mine one?' said Abou. 'Nay, not so,'
Replied the angel. Abou spoke more low,
But cheerily still; and said, 'I pray thee, then,
Write me as one that loves his fellow men.'
The angel wrote, and vanished. The next night
It came again with a great wakening light,
And showed the names whom love of God had blest,
And lo! Ben Adhem's name led all the rest.

JAMES LEIGH HUNT

To the Nile

It flows through old hushed Egypt and its sands,
Like some grave mighty thought threading a dream;
And time and things as in that vision, seem
Keeping along it their eternal stands, –
Caves, pillars, pyramids, the shepherd bands

That roam'd through the young world, the glory extreme
Of high Sesostris, and that southern beam,
The laughing queen that caught the world's great hands.
Then comes a mightier silence, stern and strong,
As of a world left empty of its throng,
And the void weighs on us, and then we wake,
And hear the fruitful stream lapsing along
'Twixt villages and think how we shall take
Our own calm journey on for human sake.

JAMES LEIGH HUNT

James Henry Leigh Hunt was born in 1784 in Middlesex, the son of an itinerant US preacher. Much of his life was spent editing, publishing and writing articles. Dickens caricatured him in the character of Harold Skimpole in *Bleak House*, focusing primarily on Hunt's ability to attract all the most notable writers to his house in Hampstead. Above all, he is remembered for introducing such writers as Shelley and Keats to the public in his highly authoritative journal *The Examiner*. He died in 1859.

Balkh, Bokhara, Samarkand

Could I ever hesitate
Balkh, Bokhara, Samarkand,
All their stir and idle state,
Sweet, to offer to thy hand.

Go and ask the Emperor
If cities can be given and got;
He is wiser, lordlier,
How men love he knoweth not.

Mighty Lord, thy hand is stayed,
Gifts like these thou puttest by;
One should have as sweet a maid,
Be a beggar poor as I.

GOETHE
as translated by E. Dowden

Favoured Animals

Promise of Paradise that spoke,
Four favoured beasts did hear;
And now with saints and pious folk
They live the eternal year.

First comes an ass with lively tread;
She takes the place of honour,
For, to the City of Prophets led,
Rode Jesus mounted on her.

Sidles a wolf with timorous air,
Whom Muhammad schooled in duty:

17

'This poor man's sheep be sure to spare,
The rich man's be your booty.'

Brisk, brave, wagging his tail, now see
With master brave, in heaven,
The little dog that faithfully
Slept with the Sleepers Seven

Here purrs Abu Huraya's cat
Round him with coaxings bland;
A holy creature sure is that
Stroked by the Prophet's hand.

GOETHE

as translated by E. Dowden

Hegira

North, South and West are rent to shivers
Thrones explode and empire quivers;
Flee to the unsullied East,
On patriarchal air to feast;
Midst love and wine, where song is sung
Old Khiser's fount shall make thee young.

There, in righteous realms and pure,
I'd plumb the spring and cynosure,
The depths whereof mankind's conceived,
Where still from Godhead they received
In earthen tongues high Heaven's lore,
And wracking of their brains forebore.

Where patriarchs they lionised,
Extraneous service they despised;

I would rejoice in youth's resort:
So vast in faith, constrained in thought,
How word was of such token there,
Because the Word was spoken there.

With herdsmen I'd associate,
Oases would refresh my state,
When in the caravan's parade
In coffee, shawls and musk I trade;
I'd walk each pathway's ups and downs
From out of the desert to the towns.

There is, on parlous cliffbound roads,
Much comfort, Hafiz, in thine odes
Whene'er the raptured head of train
High on his mule take up the strain
Of sound aloud, the stars to wake
And make the robbers' spirits quake.

I would, at inn and bathing hall,
O hallowed Hafiz, thee recall;
If sweetheart lift her veil aloft,
And shake her amber curls to waft.
The poet's lovesome whispers e'en,
They say, make Huris libertine.

I envy him this thing ye will
Begrudge him e'en, or bear it ill,
Know ye but this: that poets' verse
With quiet knocking doth traverse
For ever Paradise's portal
Supplicant for life immortal.

GOETHE
translation by S. R. Fennell

19

Ecstasy and Desire

Tell it to no-one, speak only to the wise
For the mob will only mock.
I will praise the living thing
That longs for death by fire.

On those nights of love, when your ardour
Has been slaked and cooled
Begetting as you begat,
The gleam of the silent candle
Fills you with a strange emotion.

You remain a prisoner
No longer in the shadowing darkness
And a new desire snatches
On upwards to a higher union

No distance can weigh you down
You come flying, fascinated
And at last, lusting for the light
Poor moth,
You perish in the flame.

And until you possess it,
This commandment:
Die and become!
You will be but a dismal guest
On the dark earth.

GOETHE
literal translation by J. M. Cohen

Goethe's great salute to Islamic culture was published as *West-East Divan*. For all its fame and influence it took over a century to sell out of its first print run. It forms an extraordinary supplement to his life's work, a dialogue with the work of a fourteenth-century Persian poet, Muhammad Shams-ud-Din (Hafiz), whom Goethe had only been introduced to aged sixty-five.

Johann Wolfgang von Goethe was born in 1749 in Frankfurt-am-Main, by turns playwright, poet, scientist, romantic traveller and court official to the Duke of Weimar. He never travelled east of Italy and was entirely dependent on a two-volume collection of Hafiz that had been published by Cotta in 1812–13. This translation was the work of Josef von Hammer, the son of an Austrian civil servant from Styria, who had been fortunate enough to study under the French freethinker, Thomas von Chabert, in Vienna's Oriental Academy. Josef von Hammer worked as a dragoman interpreter in Istanbul from 1799 to 1803, but his scholarly enthusiasms and liberal sympathies made him an object of suspicion to the Habsburg authorities. Later he would be employed by Metternich, though the great Austrian reactionary doubted that any poetry-lover was fit to become an ambassador. Pensioned off with the dignity of interpreter to the court at Vienna, Josef was free to devote his life to oriental literature and his multi-volume *History of the Ottoman Empire*. Goethe happily acknowledged that his own *Divan* could not have 'been thought or written' without the von Hammer translation.

Goethe was powerfully attracted by Hafiz's heartfelt celebration of wine and desire, which fitted so well with the pattern of his own life. He was beginning to feel that the hitherto strong division between an earthy sensuality and a spiritual search for the divinity was dissolving into one pantheistic unity. But unlike Hafiz we can in Goethe's case identify the cup-bearer and the beloved, for the period from 1814–15 (when he composed the *Divan*) coincided with a passionate affair with Marianne, a beautiful actress and poet, who entertained Goethe in the house of her husband, a prosperous Frankfurt banker.

In English letters Goethe is better known for his *Travels*, his romantic novel, *The Young Werther* and for *Faust*, which he worked on between 1775 and his death in 1832. He also wrote a verse in praise of the Prophet:

> behold this spring among the rocks,
> bright with joy, like a gleam of stars:
> above the clouds its youth was nurtured
> by good spirits among cliffs in the bushes.

FROM *The Veiled Prophet of Khorassan*

Upon his couch the veiled Mokanna lay,
While lamps around – not such as lend their ray,
Glimmering and cold, to those who nightly pray
In holy Koom, or Mecca's dim arcades,
But brilliant, soft, such lights as lovely maids
Look loveliest in, shed their luxurious glow
Upon his mystic Veils' white glittering flow.
Beside him, 'stead of beads and books of prayer,
Which the world fondly thought he mus'd on there,
Stood vases, fill'd with Kishmeer's golden wine,
And the red weepings of the Shiraz vine;
Of which his curtain'd lips full many a draught
Took zealously, as if each drop they quaff'd
Like Zemzem's spring of holiness, had power
To freshen the soul's virtues into flower!

*   *   *

Meanwhile, through vast illuminated halls,
Silent and bright, where nothing but the falls
Of fragrant waters, gushing with cool sound
From many a jaspar fount, is heard around,
Young Azim roams bewilder'd, nor can guess
What means this maze of light and loneliness.
Here, the way leads, o'er tessellated floors
Or mats of Cairo, through long corridors,
Where, ranged in cassolets and silver urns,
Sweet wood of aloe or of sandal burns;
And spicy rods, such as illume at night

The bowers of Tibet, send forth odorous light,
Like Peris' wands, when pointing out the road
For some pure spirit to its blest abode:
And here, at once, the glittering saloon
Bursts on his sight, boundless and bright as noon;
Where, in the midst, reflecting back the rays
In broken rainbows, a fresh fountain plays
High as the enamell'd cupola, which towers
All rich with Arabeques of gold and flowers:
And the mosaic floor beneath shines through
The sprinkling of that fountain's silvery dew,
Like the wet, glistening shells, of evry dye,
That on the margin of the Red Sea lie.

THOMAS MOORE

Whether by chance or in sympathy with Goethe, this was the same period that Thomas Moore (1779–1856) was at work on his romance *Lalla Rookh* (of which the previous poem is a part). Published by Longmans into the post-war depression of 1817, its exuberant otherworldliness and story-telling helped turn it into a great popular success, going through multiple editions in the following decades. In its final form, with line illustrations by Tenniel, chapter summaries, historical footnotes (lifted from Sale's *Koran* and Chardin's *Persian Travels*) and rich faux-Moorish binding, it became a much-loved icon of the Victorian bookshelves. It is now largely unread, though its influence, be it through popular ballads or the exotic oriental backdrops favoured by film, opera and theatre, remain with us still. This is thoroughly in keeping with Moore's own wide-ranging genius as poet, singer, songwriter, entertainer and lawyer. Born above the shop in Dublin, he was among the very first Catholics permitted into University, yet he remained in touch with the oral heritage of Ireland as the son of a Gaelic-speaking Kerryman. The toast of London society, even before his marriage to the high-profile actress Bessy Dyke, his exuberant high-living (compounded by a speculative liability) forced him to flee to Paris in 1819 – where he and his wife were befriended by Byron. His fame now rests on his Irish verse reinforced by his role as a national poet, the 'Robert Burns of Ireland'.

Kubla Khan

In Xanadu did Kubla Khan
A stately pleasure-dome decree:
Where Alph, the sacred river, ran
Through caverns measureless to man
   Down to a sunless sea.
So twice five miles of fertile ground
With walls and towers were girdled round:
And there were gardens bright with sinuous rills,
Where blossomed many an incense-bearing tree;
And here were forests ancient as the hills,
Enfolding sunny spots of greenery.

But O, that deep romantic chasm which slanted
Down the green hill athwart a cedarn cover!
A savage place! as holy and enchanted
As e'er beneath a waning moon was haunted
By woman wailing for her demon-lover!
And from this chasm, with ceaseless turmoil seething,
As if this earth in fast, thick pants were breathing,
A mighty fountain momently was forced:
Amid whose swift half-intermitted burst
Huge fragments vaulted like rebounding hail,
Or chaffy grain beneath the thresher's flail:
And 'mid these dancing rocks at once and ever
It flung up momently the sacred river.
Five miles meandering with a mazy motion
Through wood and dale the sacred river ran,
Then reached the caverns measureless to man,
And sank in tumult to a lifeless ocean:

And 'mid this tumult Kubla heard from far
Ancestral voices prophesying war!

    The shadow of the dome of pleasure
    Floated midway on the waves;
    Where was heard the mingled measure
    From the fountain and the caves.
It was a miracle of rare device,
A sunny pleasure-dome with caves of ice!

    A damsel with a dulcimer
    In a vision once I saw:
    It was an Abyssinian maid,
    And on her dulcimer she played,
    Singing of Mount Abora.
    Could I revive within me,
    Her symphony and song,
To such a deep delight 'twould win me,
That with music loud and long,
I would build that dome in air,
That sunny dome! those caves of ice!
And all who heard should see them there,
And all should cry, Beware! Beware!
His flashing eyes, his floating hair!
Weave a circle round him thrice,
And close your eyes with holy dread,
For he on honey-dew hath fed,
And drunk the milk of paradise.

SAMUEL TAYLOR COLERIDGE

After an unhappy childhood, Samuel Taylor Coleridge studied at Christ's Hospital and Jesus College, Cambridge. But it was on a walking tour that he met fellow Romantic Robert Southey, with whom he planned a 'pantisocracy' or communist society on the banks of the Susquehanna, in Pennsylvania. The idea never materialised. His earlier years were spent lecturing, writing articles and occasionally preaching in Unitarian chapels. Initially based in Bristol, it was not until 1797 that he and his wife, Sarah Fricker, moved to a cottage in Somerset and met William and Dorothy Wordsworth. Together they transformed English poetry, moving it away from neo-classical pretence. This move was signalled by their joint-work *Lyrical Ballads*, a book that opened with Coleridge's *Rime of the Ancient Mariner*. A prolific career was cut short by opium addiction, however, an ill which also cooled his friendship with the Wordsworths. He moved to London where he belatedly published *Kubla Khan* in 1816, written as it was many years earlier. He continued to write criticism right up to his death in 1834.

The Destruction of Sennacherib

The Assyrian came down like the wolf on the fold,
And his cohorts were gleaming in purple and gold;
And the sheen of his spears was like stars on the sea
When the blue wave rolls nightly on deep Galilee.

Like the leaves of the forest when Summer is green,
That host with their banners at sunset were seen:
Like the leaves of the forest when Autumn hath blown,
That lost on the morrow lay wither'd and strown.

For the Angel of Death spread his wings on the blast,
And breathed in the face of the foe as he pass'd;
And the eyes of the sleepers wax'd deadly and chill,
And their hearts but once heaved, and for ever grew still!

And there lay the steed with his nostrils all wide,
But through it there roll'd not the breath of his pride;
And the foam of his gasping lay white on the turf,
And cold as the spray of the rock beating surf.

And there lay the rider distorted and pale,
With the dew on his brow, and the rust on his mail;
And the tents were all silent, the banners alone,
The lances uplifted, the trumpet unblown.

And the widows of Ashur are loud in their wail,
And the idols are broke in the temple of Baal;
And the might of the Gentile, unsmote by the sword,
Hath melted like snow in the glance of the Lord!

GEORGE GORDON BYRON

Vision of Belshazzar

The King was on his throne,
    The Satraps thronged the hall;
A thousand bright lamps shone
    O'er that high festival.
A thousand cups of gold,
    In Judah deemed divine –
Jehovah's vessels hold
    the godless heathen's wine.

In that same hour and hall,
    The fingers of a hand
Came forth against the wall,
    And wrote as if on sand:
The fingers of a man; –
    A solitary hand
Along the letters ran,
    And traced them like a wand.

The monarch saw, and shook,
    And bade no more rejoice;
All bloodless wax'd his look,
    And tremulous his voice.
'Let the men of lore appear,
    The wisest of the earth.
And expound the words of fear,
    Which mar our royal mirth.'

Chaldea's seers are good,
    But here they have no skill;
And the unknown letters stood
    Untold and awful still.

And Babel's men of age
    Are wise and deep in lore;
But now they were not sage,
    They saw – but knew no more.

A captive in the land,
    A stranger and a youth,
He heard the king's command
    He saw that writing's truth,
The lamps around were bright,
    The prophesy in view;
He read it on that night, –
    The morrow proved it true.

'Belshazzar's grave is made
    His kingdom pass'd away,
He, in the balance weigh'd,
    Is light and worthless clay.
The shroud, his robe of state,
    His canopy the stone:
The Mede is at his gate!
    The Persian on his throne!'

GEORGE GORDON BYRON

George Gordon Byron was born in 1788 in London, in lodgings off Cavendish Square. Lame from birth, he was the son of an unintelligent, bad-tempered mother, Catherine Gordon and an entirely absent father, Captain John Byron. His father died before he could ever know him (abroad in France) when he was but three – so that his entire childhood was spent trapped with his dour Scotch mother in Aberdeen. The death of a great-uncle, aged just ten, brought him a private income, a large Gothic family house (Newstead Abbey near Nottingham) and the title of the sixth Baron Byron. The young lord was sent to Harrow School and then onto Cambridge which gave him a lifelong taste for poetry and intense relationships with boys. In 1809 he went east on a two-year journey through Albania, Greece and Turkey. A year after his return, in March 1812, the publication of *Childe Harold's Pilgrimage* and *Cantos I & II* turned him into one of the first literary celebrities. In Byron's words 'I awoke one morning and found myself famous.' Two years later *The Corsair* would sell 10,000 copies on the first day of publication, and he made his maiden speech at the House of Lords in defence of the violent strike actions of the Nottingham weavers. The first to be labelled 'mad, bad and dangerous to know', Byron was the darling of London society. His public affairs with Lady Caroline Lamb and Lady Oxford were in due course eclipsed by the very real love that he felt for his half-sister Augusta.

He left England in April 1816 to escape the threat of being prosecuted for incest and sodomy. He travelled with Shelley and his entourage of women, before cutting his own course through the fleshpots of Italy, living by turn in Venice, Ravenna and Genoa. The death of both Shelley and his own young daughter (to whom he had been an absentee father) in 1822 shocked him into abandoning his career of creative hedonism. He intensified his support for political causes, both against the oppression of the Habsburgs in Italy and for the freedom of Greece. He died of marsh fever at Missolonghi in western Greece in 1824, having joined the army of liberation as a foreign volunteer. His body was refused burial at Westminster Abbey but his spirit continued to inspire many of the creative individuals of the western world, be it Pushkin, Heine, Berlioz, Hugo, Delacroix, Garibaldi or Mazzini.

Ozymandias

I met a traveller from an antique land
Who said: Two vast and trunkless legs of stone
Stand in the desert. Near them, on the sand,
Half sunk, a shattered visage lies, whose frown,
And wrinkled lip, and sneer of cold command,
Tell that its sculptor well those passions read
Which yet survive, stamped on these lifeless things,
The hand that mocked them, and the heart that fed:
And on the pedestal these words appear:
'My name is Ozymandias, king of kings:
Look on my works, ye Mighty, and despair!'
Nothing beside remains. Round the decay
Of that colossal wreck, boundless and bare
The lone and level sands stretch far away.

PERCY BYSSHE SHELLEY

Tim Mackintosh Smith in his recent book *Travels with a Tangerine* has identified an Arabic version of 'Ozymandias'. The guidebook writer al-Harawi inscribed:

Where are the giants and emperors of old?
They and their treasure-houses none could save.
The void itself was straightened with their hosts,
As they lie straightened now within the grave.

on the chest of a statue at Luxor, then thoughtfully added a postscript: 'May God have mercy on him that pondered and drew a moral.'

Shelley never travelled down the Nile himself, and so had no opportunity to visit the two massive seated statues, the Colossi of Memnon, that stand on the west bank opposite Karnak and guide the visitor towards Medinat Habu and the ruined enclosure of the Ramasseum. Within this mortuary shrine you can recite Ozymandias whilst sitting on the colossal broken ruins of the granite statue of Rameses II. In the first century BC the Greek historian Diodurus Siculus transcribed an inscription he found here, but blurred the pharoah's praenomen (User-Maat-Re) into Ozymandias. He recorded, 'I am Ozymandias, King of Kings. If any would know how great I am, and where I lie, let him excel me in any of my works.' Shelley's celebrated reply is an attack on all autocrats, but was especially addressed to King George III and the head of Rameses that had just been unveiled in Montague House – the forerunner of the British Museum.

To the Nile

Month after month the gathered rains descend
Drenching yon secret Aethiopian dells,
And from the desert's ice-girt pinnacles
Where Frost and Heat in strange embraces blend
On Atlas, fields of moist snow half depend.
Girt there with blasts and meteors Tempest dwells
By Nile's aëreal urn, with rapid spells
Urging those waters to their mighty end.

O'er Egypt's land of memory floods are level
And they are thine, O Nile, and well thou knowest
That soul-sustaining airs and blasts of evil
And fruits and poisons spring where'er thou flowest.
Beware, O Man – for knowledge must to thee,
Like the great flood to Egypt, ever be.

PERCY BYSSHE SHELLEY

FROM THE ARABIC: *An Imitation*

I

My faint spirit was sitting in the light
    Of thy looks, my love;
It panted for thee like the hind at noon
    For the rooks, my love.
Thy barb whose hoofs outspeed the tempest's flight
    Bore thee far from me;
My heart, for my weak feet were weary soon,
    Did companion thee.

II

Ah! fleeter far than fleetest storm or steed,
    Or the death they bear,
The heart which tender thought clothes like a dove
    With the wings of care;
In the battle, in the darkness, in the need,
    Shall mine cling to thee,
Nor claim one smile for all the comfort, love,
    It may ring to thee.

PERCY BYSSHE SHELLEY

Having acquired the nickname 'Mad Shelley' during his days at Eton College, Percy Bysshe Shelley was expelled from Oxford in 1811 for his co-authorship of a pamphlet entitled 'The Necessity of Atheism'. In the years that followed, he eloped twice and settled near Windsor Great Park in 1816. That year he met Byron, his wife Harriet committed suicide and he married the other love of his life, Mary Wollstonecraft. In 1818 he moved to Italy, where he would spend the rest of his life. Shelley was as interested in politics as he was in poetry but it is his unconventional behaviour for which he is usually remembered. In 1822 a storm upturned the schooner in which he was returning from Livorno. All three men on board were drowned.

Of the Bani Udhra

Every day the lovely Princess
Came to walk beside the fountain,
Where the waters splash and sparkle,
Every day she came, at evening.

Every day the charming slave-boy
Stood at eve beside the fountain,
Where the waters splash and sparkle,
Pale he grew and ever paler.

Till one day the lovely Princess
Stepping swiftly thus approached him:
Of your name I would have knowledge,
Of your home, and of your kinsfolk.

And the slave replied: Muhammed
Is my name, my country Yemen,
And my tribe are they of Udhra,
They who die, when love assails them.

HEIDRICH HEINE (1797–1856)

This poem reaches back to an ancient tradition. It is related that Sa'id Ibn Uqba of Hamadan asked a certain bedouin, 'Of what people are you?', he replied, 'I am of those who die when they love.' Sa'id exclaimed, 'By the Lord of the Kaaba, you are of the Bani Udhra.' Then he asked, 'Why is it thus with you?' The bedouin replied: 'Our women are beautiful, and our young men are chaste.' This is mirrored by a saying of the Prophet remembered by Ibn Abbas, 'One who loves, and wins his beloved yet remains chaste and dies, dies the death of a martyr.'

from *The Robbers*

In the night, beyond the Volga
The robber gangs flocked around their fires

The crew were Cossacks and the sails were silk
At the helm, the Hetman with his gun.
At the prow, the captain with his lance.
On the deck, a tent of velvet
Shelters caskets filled with gold.
On them, stretched on silken carpets
The Hetman's doxy sleeps.
A Creature fresh as blood and milk,
All beauty, all desire

ALEXANDER PUSHKIN

from *The Fountain of Bakhchisaray*

With brooding eyes sat Khan Girey
Blue smoke his amber mouthpiece shrouded;
About their fearsome ruler crowded
The Court in sedulous array.
Deep silence reigned about the prince;
All humbly scanned the least reflection
Of irritation or dejection
On his beclouded countenance.
But now a gesture of impatience
From the imperious lord of nations
Made all bow low and melt away.

Enthroned alone remains Girey;
More freely labours now his breathing,
More clearly now his scowls betray
The surf of passion's inward seething.
Thus clouds, the brow of heaven wreathing,
Are mirrored in a changeful bay.

On what high issues is he poring?
What would his haughty mind essay?
To Russia will he fare with warring,
On Poland force his sword and sway?
Is he aflame with bloody vengeance,
Are plots uncovered in his host,
Do mountain tribes alarm him most
Or devious Genoa's subtle engines?

No – he has tired of armoured fame.
That formidable arm is tame;
The lure of stratagems has faded.

Should rank defilement have invaded
His harem on betrayal's spoor.
A child of charms enchained have traded
Her ardent heart to a giaour?

No – Girey's wives, subdued of bearing,
Designs still less than wishes daring,
In his melancholy stillness blush;
Their guard is vigilant and dreaded,
They harbour no deceit, embedded
Deep in their drear unsolaced hush.
In stealth their beauty blooms and wanes,
A sombre dungeon for its bower:

Thus blossoms of Arabia flower
Beneath the sheltering hothouse panes.
For them, disconsolately flow
Days, months, and years in changeless rhythm,
And, all unnoticed as they go,
Take youth and love and ardour with them.
Of even hue is every day,
And slow the current of the hours.
Sloth holds the Harem's life in sway,
And seldom sweet enjoyment flowers.
The youthful wives, by forced resort
To pastimes of whatever sort,
Will choose among their gorgeous raiments,
Engage in games and entertainments,
Or, deep in shade of sycamores,
By well-springs babbling near their quarters,
May sport in gauzy threes and fours,
Be-ribonned by the shining waters.
A baleful eunuch wanders here;
To counter him is vain endeavour:
His unrelenting eye and ear
Are fixed on all their movements, ever.
Their changeless orders bear his seal.
The sum and essence of his functions
Lies in his master's word and weal,
Not the august Koran's injunctions
Does he observe with greater zeal.
His soul spurns love; a graven idol
Of unconcern, he does not bridle
At hatred, scorn, reproach; he brooks
The taunts which wanton mischief utters,
Disdain, appeal, submissive looks,

Unspeaking sighs, and languid mutters.
No stranger he to women's hearts,
He knows how wily are their arts
At large or in the dungeon's throe:
Eyes melting, tears' appealing source,
Are impotent to stay his course;
He ceased to trust them long ago.

ALEXANDER PUSHKIN

Alexander Sergevich Pushkin was born in 1799. Having attended the Lyceum near St Petersburg, Pushkin soon found himself exiled to the South due to his liberalism. Only after the accession of Nicholas I was he released from confinement on his estate. His wife was Natalia Goncharova, the most beautiful woman in St Petersburg. It seems that she may have had an affair with the dashing French Baron George d'Anthès, which provoked Pushkin to challenge the man to a duel. So it was that on a cold morning in 1837 on the outskirts of St Petersburg, Russia's greatest poet was killed attempting to guard his honour. He was not yet forty.

Thanks to this poem the marble fountain in the second courtyard of the still-standing Palace of the Khan of the Crimean Tartars is ornamented each day with a fresh rose, offered up to the genius of Pushkin. The memory of the Tartar Khan's, descendants of Genghis Khan and the designated heirs to the lands of the Great Turk should the Osmanli dynasty fail, has been supplanted by that of a poet in the heart of their palace.

The Slave's Dream

Beside the ungathered rice he lay,
His sickle in his hand;
His breast was bare, his matted hair
Was buried in the sand.
Again, in the mist and shadow of sleep,
He saw his native Land.

Wide through the landscape of his dreams
The Lordly Niger flowed;
Beneath the palm-trees on the plain
Once more a king he strode;
And heard the tinkling caravans
Descend the mountain-road.

He saw once more his dark-eyed queen
Among her children stand;
They clasped his neck, they kissed his cheeks,
They held him by the hand! –
A tear burst from the sleeper's lids
And fell into the sand.

And then at furious speed he rode
Along the Niger's bank:
His bridle-reins were golden chains,
And, with a martial clank,
At each leap he could feel his scabbard of steel
Smiting his stallions's flank.

Before him, like a blood-red flag,
The bright flamingoes flew;

From morn til night he followed their flight,
O'er plains where the tamarind grew,
Till he saw the roofs of Caffre huts,
And the ocean rose to view.

At night he heard the lion roar,
And the hyena scream,
And the river-horse, as he crashed the reeds
Beside some hidden stream:
And it passed, like a glorious roll of drums,
Through the triumph of his dream.

The forests, with their myriad tongues,
Shouted of liberty;
And the Blast of the Desert cried aloud,
With a voice so wild and free,
That he started in his sleep and smiled
At their tempestuous glee.

He did not feel the driver's whip,
Nor the burning heat of day;
For death had illumined the land of sleep,
And his lifeless body lay
A worn-out fetter, that the soul
had broken and thrown away!

HENRY LONGFELLOW

Allah

(from the German of Mahlmann)

Allah gives light in darkness
   Allah gives rest in pain,
Cheeks that are white with weeping
   Allah paints red again.

The flowers and the blossoms wither
   Years vanish with flying feet;
But on my heart will live for ever,
   That here in sadness beat.

Gladly to Allah's dwelling
   Yonder would I take flight;
There will the darkness vanish,
   There will my eyes have sight.

HENRY LONGFELLOW

Henry Wadsworth Longfellow was born in Portland, Maine, in 1807. He studied at Bowdoin College in Brunswick where he attended the same classes as Nathaniel Hawthorne. He made a number of visits to Europe and in 1836 was made a Professor at Harvard University. His poetry was extremely popular during his lifetime and his skill as a storyteller is still recognised today. He died in 1882.

Extract from
Sohrab and Rustum

So, on the bloody sand, Sohrab lay dead;
And the great Rustum drew his horseman's cloak
Down o'er his face, and sate by his dead son.
As those black granite pillars, once high-rear'd
By Jemshid in Persepolis, to bear
His house, now mid their broken flights of steps
Lie prone, enormous, down the mountain's side –
So in the sand lay Rustum by his son.
And night came down over the solemn waste,
And the two gazing hosts, and that's sole pair,
And darken'd all; and a cold fog, with night,
Crept from the Oxus. Soon a hum arose,
As of a great assembly loosed, and fires
Began to twinkle through the fog: for now
Both armies moved to camp and took their meal:
The Persians took it on the open sands
Southward, the Tartars by the river marge;
And Rustum and his son were left alone.

MATTHEW ARNOLD

Matthew Arnold (1822–88) was the son of the educationalist Thomas Arnold, who as the great reforming headmaster of Rugby created the concept and practice of 'muscular Christianity' that dominated the high noon of the British Empire. Matthew followed in his father's footsteps, as an Inspector of Schools, but not in matters of faith; so much so that his poetry can be seen as a coherent attempt to create an inspirational substitute for organized religion. This extract from *Sohrab and Rustum*, (his reworking of the great Persian national myth) is typical of this great humanist project. In its subject matter, the accidental murder of the young hero Sohrab by his father Rustum, it is possible to see an affinity with his own life and passions. His acknowledged masterpiece, *Balder Dead*, deals with both the death of a son and the death of a god.

FROM *The Kasidah*

'I am truth! I am truth!' we
hear the God-drunk Gnostic cry.
'The microcosm abides in Me; Eternal
Allah's nought but I!'

Mansur was wise, but wiser they who smote
Him with the hurled stones;
And, though his blood a witness bore, no
Wisdom-might could mend his bones.

How short this Life, how long withal;
 how false its weal, how true its woes,
This fever-fit with paroxysms
 to mark its opening and its close.

And when, at length, 'Great pan is dead'
Uprose the loud and dolorous cry,
A glamour wither'd on the ground, a
Splendour faded in the sky.

Yea, Pan was dead, the nazarene came
And seized his seat beneath the sun,
The votary of the Riddle-god, whose one
Is three and three is one.

Then the lank Arab foul with sweat, the
Drainer of the camel's dug,
Gorged with his leek-green lizard's meat,
Clad in his filthy rag and rug,

Bore his fierce Allah o'er his sands and
Broke, like lava-burst, upon
The realms, where reigned pre-Adamite
Kings, where rose the grand Kayanian throne.

All Faith is false, all Faith is true: Truth
Is the shattered mirror strown
In myriad bits; while each believes his little
Bit the whole to own.

Richard Burton is the quintessential British travel-writer who, like many of this breed, was educated abroad. As a young man in the Indian Service he was trained in adversity at Sind, on the Somali coast and as a staff-officer of irregular cavalry during the Crimean War. He later took the pilgrimage to Mecca in disguise, searched for the source of the Nile and served as a consul in South America, Damascus and Trieste. A restless, provoking genius, 'he finished filling in the last gaps of the geographical knowledge of the nineteenth century as he had already started on the great quest of the twentieth century, the exploration of the mysterious workings of the human mind'. It is however curious that as one of the acclaimed scholars of oral history, such as his celebrated edition of *The Thousand and One Nights*, his own books lack a lightness of touch and story-telling charm. His anonymous philosophical poem, *The Kasidah*, though wrapped in a disguise of mysticsm, speculative mythology and an eastern identity, is yet one of the most English of all his works; a pantheistic, melancholic 'cry of a soul, wandering through space, looking for what it does not find'.

Former Life

Long have I lived beneath vast porticoes
By many ocean-sunsets singed and fired;
Where mighty pillars, in celestial rows,
Stood like basaltic caves as day expired.

The waves a heavenly likeness thundered forth,
Their solemn music turbulence was brewing;
As surging harmonies of rise and cadence
Reflected evening colours in my eyes.

'Twas thus I lived in pure tranquillity,
Amid the sensual feast of sky and sea,
Of naked slaves, their bodies perfumed through,

Who cooled my languid brow with fronds of palm,
Their sole concern throughout unmodified,
To learn the secret grief that caused my pain.

CHARLES BAUDELAIRE

Charles Baudelaire was born in Paris in 1821. A poet who sought
to explore the furthest recesses of the human psyche, his first
major collection, *Les Fleurs du Mal*, was rejected by the *Académie
Française* in 1862, on the grounds that it was indecent and
blasphemous. *La Vie Antérieure* (Former Life) first appeared in
the *Revue des Deux Mondes* in 1853 but was later included in a
revised version of *Les Fleurs du Mal*. The escapist vision of the
poem is partly attributed to Baudelaire's encounter with opium,
an experience which was the subject of another of his poems, *Le
Poison*. He spent nearly all of his life in Paris, dying there in 1867.

Dream

I

With camel's hair I clothed my skin,
I fed my mouth with honey wild;
And set me scarlet wool to spin,
And all my breast with hyssop filled;
Upon my brow and cheeks and chin
A bird's blood spilled.

I took a broken reed to hold,
I took a sponge of gall to press;
I took weak water-weeds to fold
About my sacrificial dress.

I took the grasses of the field,
The flax was bolled upon my crine;
And ivy thorn and wild grapes healed
To make good wine.

I took my scrip of manna sweet,
My cruse of water did I bless;
I took the white dove by the feet,
And flew into the wilderness.

II

The tiger came and played;
Uprose the lion in his mane;
The jackal's tawny nose
And sanguine dripping tongue
Out of the desert rose
And plunged its sands among;
The bear came striding o'er the desert lain.

Uprose the horn and eyes
And quivering flank of the great unicorn,
And galloped round and round;
Uprose the gleaming claw
Of the leviathan, and wound
In steadfast march did draw
Its course away beyond the desert's bourn.

I stood within a maze
Woven round about me by a magic art,
And ordered circle-wise;
The bear more near did tread,
And with two fiery eyes,
And with a wolfish head,
Did close the circle round in every part.

III

With scarlet corded horn,
With frail wrecked knees and stumbling pace,
The scapegoat came:
His eyes took flesh and spirit dread in flame
At once, and he died looking towards my face.

RICHARD WATSON DIXON

Born in Islington in 1833 to a Wesleyan minister, Richard Watson Dixon was ordained as an Anglican curate in 1858. His better poems achieve an intensity of vision that very few other Victorians achieved in religious literature. Dixon died in 1900.

The Oasis of Sidi Khaled

How the earth burns! Each pebble underfoot
Is as a living thing with power to wound
The white sand quivers, and the footfall mute
Of the slow camels strikes but gives no sound
As though they walked on flame, not solid ground.
'Tis noon, and the beasts' shadows even have fled
Back to their feet, and there is fire around
And fire beneath, and overhead the sun.
Pitiful heaven! What is this we view?
Tall trees, a river, pools where swallows fly,
Thickets of oleander where doves coo,
Shades, deep as midnight, greenness for tired eyes.
Hark, how the light winds in the palm-tops sigh.
Oh this is rest. Oh this is paradise.

WILFRID SCAWEN BLUNT

W. S. Blunt was born in 1840 and served as a diplomat
from 1859 to 1870. He explored the Near and Middle
East, taking up such political causes as Egyptian
nationalism, before returning to England. He stood
for Parliament and was imprisoned in 1888 for his
involvement with the Irish Land League. He loved
travelling and had a great regard for the bedouin and for
pure-bred Arab horses, a passion shared by his wife,
Lady Anna Isabel Noel. He died in 1922.

A Maid for a Khan

The almond-groves of Samarcand,
　Bokhara, where red-lilies blow,
And Oxus, by whose yellow sand
　The grave white-turbaned merchants go:

And on from thence to Ispahan,
　The gilded garden of the sun,
Whence the long dusty caravan
　Brings cedar wood and vermilion;

And that dread city of Cabool
　Set at the mountains scarpèd feet,
Where marble tanks are ever full
　With water for the noonday heat:

Where through the narrow straight bazaar
　A little maid Circassian
Is led, a present from the Czar
　Unto some old and bearded khan, –

from 'Ave Imperatrix' by
OSCAR WILDE

Oscar Wilde was born in 1854 in Dublin. There he attended Dublin College before moving on to Magdalen College, Oxford. Here Wilde proved himself to be an accomplished classicist and distinguished poet. In 1882 he gave lectures throughout the States. He would later boast, 'I have civilized America.' Contemptuous of conventional morality, his private life came under the public eye at the turn of the century. After two celebrated court cases he was jailed for sodomy. The last few years of his life were spent wandering the Continent, his reputation in England now ruined. He died on Paris's Left Bank in 1900.

Arab Love-Song

The hunched camels of the night
Trouble the bright
And silver waters of the moon.
The Maiden of the Morn will soon
through Heaven stray and sing,
Star gathering.

Now while the dark about our love is strewn,
Light of my dark, blood of my heart, O come!
And the night will catch her breath up, and be dumb.

Leave thy father, leave thy mother
And thy brother;
Leave the black tents of thy tribe apart!
Am I not thy father and thy brother,
And thy mother?
And thou – what needest with thy tribe's black tents
Who hast the red pavilion of my heart?

FRANCIS THOMPSON

Francis Thompson, born in Preston, Lancashire, in 1859, was brought up in the Roman Catholic faith. He failed in his attempts to train for the priesthood or to study medicine, finally moving to London where extreme poverty led him into opium addiction. He was rescued by Wilfrid and Alice Meynell, who looked after him until his death from tuberculosis in 1907. Aside from his richly imaginative poetry, two essays on Shelley and St Ignatius Loyola were published posthumously.

FROM *Hassan – a verse-play*

Thy dawn, O Master of the world, thy dawn;
The hour the lilies open on the lawn,
The hour the grey wings pass beyond the mountains,
The hour of silence, when we hear the fountains,
The hour that dreams are brighter and winds colder,
The hour that young love wakes on a white shoulder,
O Master of the world, the Persian Dawn.
That hour, O master, shall be bright for thee:
Thy merchants chase the morning down the sea,
The braves who fight thy war unsheathe the sabre,
The slaves who work thy mines are lashed to labour,
For thee the wagons of the world are drawn –
The ebony of night, the red of dawn!

JAMES ELROY FLECKER

The Old Ships

I have seen old ships sail like swans asleep
Beyond the village which men still call Tyre,
With leaden age o'ercargoed, dipping deep
For Famagusta and the hidden sun
That rings black Cyprus with a lake of fire;
And all those ships were certainly so old
Who knows how oft with squat and noisy gun,
Questing brown slaves or Syrian oranges,
The pirates Genoese
Hell-raked them till they rolled
Blood, water, fruit and corpses up the hold.
But now through friendly seas they softly run,
Painted the mid-sea blue or, shore-sea green,
Still patterned with the vine and grapes in gold.

But I have seen,
Pointing her shapely shadows from the dawn
And image tumbled on a rose-swept bay,
A drowsy ship of some yet older day;
And, wonder's breath indrawn,
Thought I – who knows – who knows – but in that same
(Fished up beyond Æéa, patched up new
 – stern painted brighter blue –)
That talkative, bald-headed seaman came
(Twelve patient comrades sweating at the oar)
From Troy's doom-crimson shore,
And with great lies about his wooden horse
Set the crew laughing, and forgot his course.
It was so old a ship – who knows, who knows?

– And yet so beautiful, I watched in vain
To see the mast burst open with a rose,
And the whole deck put on its leaves again.

JAMES ELROY FLECKER

The Golden Journey to Samarkand

PROLOGUE

We who with songs beguile your pilgrimage
And swear that Beauty lives though lilies die,
We poets of the proud lineage
Who sing to find your hearts, we know not why, –

What shall we tell? Tales, marvellous tales
Of ships and stars and isles where good men rest,
Where nevermore the rose of sunset pales,
And winds and shadows fall toward the West:

And there the world's first huge white-bearded kings
In dim glades sleeping, murmur in their sleep,
And closer round their breast the ivy clings,
Cutting its pathway slow and red and deep.

II

And how beguile you? Death has no repose
Warmer and deeper than that Orient sand
Which hides the beauty and bright faith of those
Who made the Golden Journey to Samarkand.

And now they wait and whiten peaceably,
Those conquerors, those poets, those so fair:

They know time comes, not only you and I,
But the whole world shall whiten, here or there;

When those long caravans that cross the plain
With dauntless feet and sound of silver bells
Put forth no more for glory or for gain,
Take no more solace from the palm-girt wells.

When the great markets by the sea shut fast
All that calm Sunday that goes on and on:
When even lovers find their peace at last,
And Earth is but a star, that once had shone.

JAMES ELROY FLECKER

FROM *The Masque of the Magi*

MARY

But who are you, bright kings?

CASPAR

Caspar am I: the rocky North
From storm and silence drove me forth
    Down to the blue and tideless sea.
I do not fear the tinkling sword,
For I am a great battle-lord,
And love the horns of chivalry.
And I have brought thee splendid gold,
The strong man's joy, refined and cold.
    All hail, thou Prince of Galilee!

BALTHAZAR

I am Balthazar, Lord of Ind,
Where blows a soft and scented wind
   From Taprobane toward Cathay.
My children, who are tall and wise,
Stand by a tree with shutten eyes
     And seem to meditate or pray.
And these red drops of frankincense
Betoken man's intelligence.
     Hail, Lord of Wisdom, Prince of Day!

MELCHIOR

I am the dark man, Melchior,
And I shall live but little more
   Since I am old and feebly move.
My kingdom is a burnt-up land
Half buried by the drifting sand,
   So hot Apollo shines above.
What could I bring but simple myrrh
White blossom of the cordial fire?
     Hail, Prince of Souls and Lord of Love!

JAMES ELROY FLECKER

Saadabad

I

Let us deal kindly with a heart of old by sorrow torn:
Come with Nedim to Saadabad, my love, this silver morn:
I hear the boatmen singing from our caïque on the Horn,
Waving cypress, waving cypress, let us go to Saadabad!

We shall watch the Sultan's fountains ripple, rumble,
                                   splash and rise
Over terraces of marble, under the blue balconies,
Leaping through the plaster dragon's hollow mouth and
                                   empty eyes;
Waving cypress, waving cypress, let us go to Saadabad.

Lie a little to your mother: tell her you must out to pray,
And we'll slink along the alleys, thieves of all a summer day,
Down to the worn old watersteps, and then, my love, away
O my cypress, waving cypress, let us go to Saadabad.

You and I, and with us only some poor lover in a dream:
I and you – perhaps some minstrel who will sing beside
                                   the stream.
Ah Nedim will be the minstrel, and the lover be Nedim,
Waving cypress, waving cypress, when we go to Saadabad!

II

Down the Horn Constantinople fades and flashes in the blue,
Rose of cities dropping with the heavy summer's burning dew,
Fading now as falls the Orient evening round the sky and you,
Fading into red and silver as we row to Saadabad.

Banish then, O Grecian eyes, the passion of the waiting West!
Shall God's holy monks not enter on a day God knoweth best
To crown the Roman king again, and hang a cross upon
                                        his breast?
Daughter of the Golden Islands, come away to Saadabad.

And a thousand swinging steeples shall begin as they began
When Heraclius rode home from the wreck of Ispahan,
Naked captives pulled behind him, double eagles in the van –
But is that a tale for lovers on the way to Saadabad?

Rather now shall you remember how of old two such as we,
You like her the laughing mistress of a poet, him or me,
Came to find the flowery lawns that give the soul tranquillity:
Let the boatmen row no longer – for we land at Saadabad.

See you not that moon-dipped caïque with the lovers at
                                        the prow,
Straining eyes and aching lips, and touching hands as we
                                        do now,
See you not the turbaned shadows passing, whence?
                                        and moving, how?
Are the ghosts of all the Moslems floating down to Saadabad?

                    *   *   *

Broken fountains, phantom waters, nevermore to glide
                                        and gleam
From the dragon-mouth is plaster sung of old by old Nedim,
Beautiful and broken fountains, keep you still your
                                        Sultan's dream,
Or remember how his poet took a girl to Saadabad?

                                        JAMES ELROY FLECKER

The Hammam Name

(from the Turkish poem by Beligh)

Winsome torment rose from slumber, rubbed his eyes,
                                        and went his way
Down the street towards the Hammam. Goodness
                                        gracious! people say
What a handsome countenance! The sun has risen
                                        twice today!
And as for the Undressing Room it quivered in dismay.
With the glory of his presence see the window panes
                                        perspire,
And the water in the basin boils and bubbles with desire.

Now his lovely cap is treated like a lover: off it goes!
Next his belt the boy unbuckles; down it falls, and at his toes
All the growing heap of garments buds and blossoms
                                        like a rose.
Last of all his shirt came flying. Ah, I tremble to disclose
How the shell came off the almond, how the lily showed
                                        its face,
How I saw a silver mirror taken flashing from its case.

He was gazed upon so hotly that his body grew too hot,
So the bathman seized the adorers and expelled them
                                        on the spot;
Then the desperate shampooer his propriety forgot,
Stumbled when he brought the pattens, fumbled when
                                        he tied a knot,
And replied when musky towels had obscured his idol's hips,
See love's Plenilune, Mashallah, in a partial eclipse!

Desperate the loofah wriggled: soap was melted instantly:
All the bubble hearts were broken. Yes, for them as well as me,
Bitterness was born of beauty; as for the shampooer, he
Fainted, till a jug of water set the Captive Reason free.
Happy bath! The baths of heaven cannot wash their
                                  spotted moon:
You are doing well with this one. Not a spot upon him soon!

Now he leaves the luckless bath for fear of setting it alight;
Seizes on a yellow towel growing yellower in fright,
Polishes the pearly surface till it burns disastrous bright,
And a bathroom window shatters in amazement at the sight.
Like the fancies of a dreamer frail and soft his garments shine
As he robes a mirror body shapely as a poet's line.

Now upon his cup of coffee see the lips of Beauty bent:
And they perfume him with incense and they sprinkle
                                  him with scent,
Call him Bey and call him Pasha, and receive with deep content
The gratuities he gives them, smiling and indifferent.
Out he goes: the mirror strains to kiss her darling; out he goes!
Since the flame is out, the water can but freeze.
                            The water froze.

JAMES ELROY FLECKER

The original of this last poem is by the eighteenth-century
Turkish poet Beligh. *The Hammam Name* were first translated
into English by E. J. W. Gibbs, but Gibbs's bears no comparison
with the Flecker version.

War Song of the Saracens

We are they who come faster than fate: we are they who
        ride early or late:
We storm at your ivory gate: Pale kings of the
        Sunset, beware!
Not on silk nor in samet we lie, not in curtained
        solemnity die
Among women who chatter and cry, and children
        who mumble a prayer.
But we sleep by the ropes of the camp, and we rise with
        a shout, and we tramp
With the sun or the moon for a lamp, and the spray
        of the wind in our hair.

From the lands where the elephants are, to the forts of
        Merou and Balghar,
Our steel we have brought and our star to shine on the
        ruins of Rum.
We have marched from the Indus to Spain, and by God
        we will go there again;
We have stood on the shore of the plain where the
        Waters of Destiny boom.
A mart of destruction we made at Jalula where men
        were afraid,
For death was a difficult trade and the sword was a
        broker of doom;

And the spear was a Desert Physician who cured not a
        few of ambition,

And drave not a few to perdition with medicine bitter
                                        and strong:
And the shield was a grief to the fool and as bright as
                                        a desolate pool,
And as straight as the rock of Stamboul when their
                                        cavalry thundered along:
For the coward was drowned with the brave when
                                        our battle sheered up like a wave,
And the dead to the desert we gave, and the glory to
                                        God in our song.

JAMES ELROY FLECKER

Born in 1884, James Elroy Flecker studied at Uppingham and Trinity College, Oxford. After a brief stint as a teacher, he entered the British Consular Service and went to Cambridge to study Oriental languages. His work would take him to Istanbul, Smyrna (Izmir) and then Beirut. But although he liked to romanticise Levantine history and custom in his verse, his own encounters with the East could be jaded by personal animosity.

Flecker's many letters betray the intensity of his passion for his art. As a poet he was chiefly concerned with achieving beauty in his writings, but he identified with the French Parnassians rather than the Romantics, seeing the latter as too keen to convey a message. 'It is not the poet's business to save man's soul but to make it worth saving . . . ' he said. His works were published in the last five years of his life. He died at the age of thirty.

The Word and Silence

If words have no meaning, silence is precious
                              – traditional Arabic proverb

Silence is golden and the word is silver.

What profane one pronounced such blasphemy?
What sluggish Asian blind and mute resigned to
blind mute destiny? What wretched madman,
a stranger to humanity, insulting virtue
called the son chimera and the word silver?
Our only god-befitting gift, containing all –
enthusiasm, sorrow, joy, love;
our only human trait in our bestial nature!
You who call it silver do not have faith
in the future that will dissolve silences, mysterious word.
You do not luxuriate in wisdom, progress does not charm you;
with ignorance – golden silence – you are pleased.
You are ill. Unfeeling silence is a grave disease;
while the warm sympathetic Word is health.
Silence is shadow and night, the Word is daylight.
The Word is truth, life, immortality.
Let us speak, let us speak – silence does not suit us
since we have been created in the image of the Word.
Let us speak, let us speak – since within us speaks
divine thought, the soul's unbodied speech.

CONSTANTINE CAFAVY

Sham-el-Nessim
(Breathing the Breeze)

Our pallid Egypt
the sun scorches and scourges
with bitter- and spite-laden arrows
and exhausts it with thirst and disease.
Our sweet Egypt
in a gay fair
gets drunk, forgets, and adorns itself, and rejoices
and scorns the tyrannical sun.

Joyous Shem-el-Nessim, innocent country festival,
announces the spring.
Alexandria with her many dense roads empties.
The good Egyptian wants to celebrate
the joyous Sham-el-Nessim and he becomes a nomad.
From everywhere pour out

the battalions of holiday lovers. The Khabari fills
and the blue-green, musing Mahmoudiya.
The Mex, Muharram Bey, the Ramleh are jammed.
And the countrysides compete to see which will get
the most carts, loaded with happy people, arriving
in solemn, serene merriment.

For the Egyptian preserves his solemnity
even at the festival;
he adorns his fez with flowers but his face
is immobile. He murmurs a monotonous song
with gaiety. There is much good spirit in his thoughts,
least in his movements.

Our Egypt has no rich greenness,
          no delightful creeks or fountains,
it has no high mountains that cast a broad shade.
But it has magic flowers fallen aflame
from the torch of Ptah; exhaling unknown fragrance,
          aromas in which nature swoons.

Amid a circle of admirers the sweet singer of the
          widest fame is warmly applauded;
in his tremulous voice pains of love
sigh; his song bitterly complains
of the fickle Fatma or cruel Emineh,
          of the wiliest Zeinab.

With the shaded tents and the cold sherbet,
          the scorching heat and dust are routed.
The hours pass like moments, like steeds hastening
over the smooth plain and their gleaming manes
fanning out gaily over the festival
          gild the joyous Sham-el-Nessim.

          Our pallid Egypt
          the sun scorches and scourges
with bitter- and spite-laden arrows
and exhausts it with thirst and disease.
          Our sweet Egypt
          in a gay festival
gets drunk, forgets, and adorns itself, and rejoices
and scorns the tyrannical sun.

CONSTANTINE CAFAVY

In Harbour

A young man, twenty-eight years of age, Emes arrived
at this little Syrian harbour on a tenion vessel
with the intention of learning to be a perfume seller.
But during the voyage he fell ill; and as soon
as he disembarked, he died. His burial, the very poorest,
took place here. A few hours before he died,
he murmured something about 'home', about 'very
                                    old parents'.
But who they were nobody knew,
nor which his country in the vast panhellenic world.
It is better so. For in this way, though
he lies dead in this little harbour,
his parents will always go on hoping he is alive.

CONSTANTINE CAFAVY

Their Beginning

The fulfilment of their deviate, sensual delight
Is done. They rose from the mattress,
And they dress hurriedly without speaking.
They leave the house separately, furtively; and as
They walk somewhat uneasily on the street, it seems
As if they suspect that something about them betrays
Into what kind of bed they fell a little while back.

But how the life of the artist has gained.
Tomorrow, the next day, years later, the vigorous verses
Will be composed that had their beginning here.

CONSTANTINE CAFAVY

Constantine Cafavy (1863–1933) has a place in the pantheon of Greek poets but his unique voice has also endeared him to the wider world. He was the youngest son of a charismatic Greek merchant, who had been born in Constantinople but had moved to Alexandria in 1850 at the same time that his elder brother had expanded the family firm of Cafay & Sons by setting up branches in England. Apart from seven years spent in England, after the death of his father, Constantine lived, dreamed and worked (as a civil servant and occasional stockbroker) within the metropolitan confines of Alexandria. He inhabited particularly a triangular grid of street-pavements that connected his office, apartment and neighbourhood café where a group of friends awaited him, to watch him sip Turkish coffee and talk, with equal ease in Greek, English or French. His mother, Chariclea, was descended from a Phanariot family (the Greek intellectuals who worked as government officials within the Ottoman Empire). This may have encouraged him to pursue his imaginative reveries through the vast thoroughfares and forgotten byways of the Hellenic past, touched now and then by the scent of crumpled sheets left behind by an afternoon in a bedroom. His reflections on the Arab and Egyptian world that he existed amongst are not so well known. Both *The Word and Silence* and *Sham-el-Nessim* were early works which he would later try to suppress. *In Harbour* and *Their Beginning* are much more characteristic.

PART TWO

POEMS FROM THE EAST

✳

FROM *The Song of Solomon*
(Chapter 2:10–13)

My beloved spake, and said unto me, Rise up, my love,
                    my fair one, and come away.
For lo, the winter is past, the rain is over, and gone;
The flowers appear on the earth, the time of the singing of
birds is come, and the voice of the turtle is heard
                                        in our land;
The fig tree putteth forth her green figs, and the vines
                    with the tender grape give a good smell.
Arise, my love, my fair one, and come away.

KING JAMES BIBLE

Born in 1015 BC, Solomon ruled over the Jews when their
kingdom was at its apogee. Blessed with extraordinary
wisdom and fabulous wealth, he built the great temple to
Jehovah in Jerusalem but displeased his God by keeping
foreign women in his harem. The discontent bred by his
over-taxation divided his kingdom in half after his death.
As well as the *Song of Solomon*, the books of *Ecclesiastes*
and *Proverbs* are usually attributed to him.

The Lament to Dassine, Famed Poetess

Like thou, O Dassine-oult-Yemma
death in battle has preferred other than I
and for the lion's share has chosen

Djeloul, whose head was broken by a club;

Mechedgi, blinded by a dagger
seeks in his madness to find the sun;

Ebeggi whose heart was opened
by a scimitar as an orange is opened with a knife;

Akelaoui, whose entrails
lay like red serpents in the sand;

Boulkadjmi,
nailed to the sands by spears
two through the hands and two through the feet
and whose belly became swollen
like a rounded shield in the sun.

THE AMENOUKAL OF THE HOGGAR

Dassine was a Tuareg noblewoman living in the Hoggar at the beginning of the twentieth century. Her beauty was renowned throughout the Sahara. Many a noble Tuareg tried to win her love and failed. This verse is addressed to her by the paramount chief of one of the four Tuareg 'kingdoms' of the central Sahara.

The Arabian Nights, or *The Thousand and One Nights* (*Alf Layla wa-Layla*) as it is known in the Arabic world, is a collection of stories probably based on the Persian *Hazar Afsaneh* (*Thousand Stories*) and enriched by tales from the Cairo streets. The earliest surviving fragment of the Arabic version dates from the ninth century.

Hunger

Wail for the little partridges on porringer and plate;
Cry for the ruin of the fries and stews well marinate:
Keen as I keen for loved lost daughters of the sand-grouse,
And omelette round the fair embrowned fowls agglomerate:
O fire in heart of me for fish, those *deux poissons* I saw
Bedded on new-baked flat bread and cakes in piles to laniate.

For thee, O vermicelli! aches my very maw! I hold
Without thee every taste and joy are clean annihilate.
Those eggs have rolled their yellow eyes in torturing pains of fire
Ere served with hash and fritters not, their delicatest cate.
Praised be Allah for his baked and roast and ah! how good
This pulse, these pot-herbs steeped on oil with eysill combinate.

When hunger sated was, I elbowed-propt fell back upon
Meat-puddings where in gleamed the bangles that my wits amate.
Then woke I sleeping appetite to eat as though in sport
Sweets from brocaded trays and kickshaws most elaborate.
Be patient, soul of me! Time is haughty, jealous wight;
Today he seems dark-lowering and tomorrow fair to sight.

from *The Arabian Nights* translated by
RICHARD BURTON

Travel

Travel! and thou shalt find new friends for old ones
                                        left behind;
Toil! for the sweets of human life by toil and moil are found:
The stay-at-home no honour wins nor aught attains
                                        but want;
So leave thy place of birth and wander all the world around!
I've seen and very oft I've seen, how standing water stinks,
And only flowing sweetens it and trotting makes it sound;
And were the moon forever full and ne'er to wax and wane,
Man would not strain his watchful eyes to see its
                                        gladsome round:
Except the lion leave the bow ne'er had it reached its bound:
Gold-dust is dust the while it lies untravelled in the mine,
And aloes-wood mere fuel is upon its native ground:
And gold shall win his highest worth when from his
                                        goal ungoal'd;
And aloes sent to foreign parts grow costlier than gold.

from *The Arabian Nights* translated by
RICHARD BURTON

Richard Francis Burton, having mastered Hindustani,
Persian and Arabic, made a pilgrimage to Mecca in 1853
disguised as a Pathan, which he wrote about in his
*Personal Narrative of a Pilgrimage to Al Madinah and
Mecca.* He spoke over forty languages and dialects and
wrote over forty books.

Song of the Minstrels of Kairouan
on a Wedding Night

Tread, tread, O my joy
Unite me to my beloved.
By Allah we will intoxicate ourselves.
Under the jasmine tree we will acquaint
                              ourselves with rapture
and none shall reproach us.
Tread, tread, O my joy!
Allah hath ordained our sweet madness!

as translated by DAHRIS MARTIN
in *Among the Faithful*

The Seven Ages of Woman

At Ten – a shelled almond sweet in men's sight:
At Fifteen – a plaything for lovers' delight :
At Twenty – cuddlesome, rounded and fat :
At Thirty – a mother with many a brat
At Forty – a crone, with no more life in her :
At fifty – 'twere better to stick a knife in her
At sixty – decrepit in body and mind, cursed by
            Allah, the Angels and all mankind.

by 'UBAYD ZÁKÁNI
taken from *Weekend Caravan*
compiled by S. Hillelson

The Rubáiyát of Omar Khayyám

Awake! for Morning in the Bowl of Night
Has flung the Stone that puts the Stars to Flight:
  And Lo! the Hunter of the East has caught
The Sultan's Turret in a Noose of Light.

Dreaming when Dawn's Left Hand was in the Sky
I heard a voice within the Tavern cry,
  'Awake, my Little ones, and fill the Cup
Before Life's Liquor in its Cup be dry.'

And, as the Cock crew, those who stood before
The Tavern shouted – 'Open then the Door!
  You know how little while we have to stay,
And, once departed, may return no more.'

Now the New Year reviving old Desires,
The thoughtful Soul to Solitude retires,
  Where the White Hand of Moses on the Bough
Puts out, and Jesus from the Ground suspires.

Iram indeed is gone with all its Rose,
And Jamshýd's Sev'n-ring'd Cup where no one knows;
  But still the Vine her ancient ruby yields,
And still a Garden by the Water blows.

And David's Lips are lock't; but in divine
High piping Pehleví, with 'Wine! Wine! Wine!
  Red Wine!' – the Nightingale cries to the Rose
That yellow Cheek of hers to incarnadine.

Come, fill the Cup, and in the Fire of Spring
The Winter Garment of Repentance fling:
  The Bird of Time has but a little way
To fly – and Lo! the Bird is on the Wing.

And look – a thousand Blossoms with the Day
Woke – and a thousand scatter'd into Clay:
  And this first Summer Month that brings the Rose
Shall take Jamshýd and Kaikobád away.

But come with old Khayyám, and leave the Lot
Of Kaikobád and Kaikhosrú forgot:
  Let Rustum lay about him as he will,
Or Hátim Tai cry Supper – heed them not.

With me along some Strip of Herbage strown
That just divides the desert from the sown,
  Where name of Slave and Sultan scarce is known,
And pity Sultan Mahmud on his Throne.

Here with a Loaf of Bread beneath the Bough,
A Flask of Wine, a Book of Verse – and Thou
  Beside me singing in the Wilderness –
And Wilderness is Paradise enow.

'How sweet is mortal Sovranty!' – think some:
Others – 'How blest the Paradise to come!'
  Ah, take the Cash in hand and waive the Rest;
Oh, the brave Music of a *distant* Drum!

Look to the Rose that blows about us – 'Lo,
Laughing,' she says, 'into the World I blow:
  At once the silken Tassel of my Purse
Tear, and its Treasure on the Garden throw.'

The Worldly Hope men set their Hearts upon
Turns Ashes – or it prospers; and anon,
   Like Snow upon the Desert's dusty Face
Lightning a little Hour or two – is gone.

And those who husbanded the Golden Grain,
And those who flung it to the Winds like Rain,
   Alike to no such aureate Earth are turn'd
As, buried once, Men want dug up again.

Think, in this batter'd Caravanserai
Whose Doorways are alternate Night and Day,
   How Sultan after Sultan with his Pomp
Abode his Hour or two and went his way.

They say the Lion and the Lizard keep
The Courts where Jamshýd gloried and drank deep:
   And Bahrám, that great Hunter – the Wild Ass
Stamps o'er his Head, and he lies fast asleep.

I sometimes think that never blows so red
The Rose as where some buried Cæsar bled;
   That every Hyacinth the Garden wears
Dropt in its Lap from some once lovely Head.

And this delightful Herb whose tender Green
Fledges the River's Lip on which we lean –
   Ah, lean upon it lightly! for who knows
From what once lovely Lip it springs unseen!

Ah, my Belovéd, fill the Cup that clears
Today of past Regrets and future Fears –
   Tomorrow? – Why, Tomorrow I may be
Myself with Yesterday's Sev'n Thousand Years.

Lo! some we loved, the lovliest and best
That Time and Fate of all their Vintage prest,
     Have drunk their Cup a Round or two before,
And one by one crept silently to Rest.

And we, that now make merry in the Room
They left, and Summer dresses in new Bloom,
     Ourselves must we beneath the Couch of Earth
Descend, ourselves to make a Couch – for whom?

Ah, make the most of what we yet may spend,
Before we too into the Dust descend;
     Dust into Dust, and under Dust, to lie,
Sans Wine, sans Song, sans Singer, and – sans End!

Alike for those who for Today prepare,
And those that after a Tomorrow stare,
     A Muezzin from the Tower of Darkness cries,
'Fools! your Reward is neither Here nor There!'

Why, all the Saints and Sages who discuss'd
Of the Two Worlds so learnedly, are thrust
     Like foolish Prophets forth; their Words to Scorn
Are scatter'd, and their Mouths are stopt with Dust.

Oh, come with old Khayyám, and leave the Wise
To talk; one thing is certain, that Life flies;
     One thing is certain, and the Rest is Lies;
The Flower that once has blown for ever dies.

Myself when young did eagerly frequent
Doctor and Saint, and heard great Argument
     About it and about; but evermore
Came out by the same Door as in I went.

With them the Seed of Wisdom did I sow,
And with my own hand labour'd it to grow:
    And this was all the Harvest that I reap'd –
'I came like Water and like Wind I go.'

Into this Universe, and *why* not knowing,
Nor *whence*, like Water willy-nilly flowing:
    And out of it, as Wind along the Waste,
I know not *whither,* willy-nilly blowing.

What, without asking, hither hurried *whence*?
And, without asking, *whither* hurried hence!
    Another and another Cup to drown
The Memory of this Impertinence!

Up from Earth's Centre through the Seventh Gate
I rose, and on the Throne of Saturn sate,
    And many Knots unravel'd by the Road;
But not the Knot of Human Death and Fate.

There was a Door to which I found no Key:
There was a Veil past which I could not see:
    Some little Talk awhile of Me and Thee
There seemed – and then no more of Thee and Me.

Then to the rolling Heav'n itself I cried,
Asking, 'What Lamp had Destiny to guide
    Her little Children stumbling in the Dark?'
And – 'A blind Understanding!' Heav'n replied.

Then to this earthen Bowl did I adjourn
My Lip the secret Well of Life to learn:
    And Lip to Lip it murmur'd – 'While you live
Drink! – for once dead you never shall return.'

I think the Vessel, that with fugitive
Articulation answer'd, once did live,
    And merry-make; and the cold Lip I kiss'd
How many Kisses might it take – and give!

For in the Marketplace, one Dusk of Day,
I watch'd the Potter thumping his wet Clay:
    And with its all obliterated Tongue
It murmur'd – 'Gently, Brother, gently, pray!'

Ah, fill the Cup – what boots it to repeat
How Time is slipping underneath our Feet:
    Unborn Tomorrow, and dead Yesterday,
Why fret about them if Today be sweet!

One Moment in Annihilation's Waste,
One Moment, of the Well of Life to taste –
    The Stars are setting and the Caravan
Starts for the Dawn of Nothing – Oh, make haste!

How long, how long, in infinite Pursuit
Of This and That endeavour and dispute?
    Better be merry with the fruitful Grape
Than sadden after none, or bitter, Fruit.

You know, my Friends, how long since in my House
For a new Marriage I did make Carouse:
    Divorced old barren Reason from my Bed,
And took the Daughter of the Vine to Spouse.

For 'Is' and 'Is-not' though *with* Rule and Line,
And 'Up-and-down' *without* I could define,
    I yet in all I only cared to know,
Was never deep in anything but – Wine.

And lately, by the Tavern Door agape,
Came stealing through the Dusk an Angel Shape
    Bearing a Vessel on his Shoulder; and
He bid me taste of it; and 'twas – the Grape!

The Grape that can with Logic absolute
The Two-and-Seventy jarring Sects confute:
    The subtle Alchemist that in a Trice
Life's leaden Metal into Gold transmute.

The mighty Mahmud, the victorious Lord,
That all the misbelieving and black Horde
    Of Fears and Sorrows that infest the Soul
Scatters and slays with his enchanted Sword.

But leave the Wise to wrangle, and with me
The Quarrel of the Universe let be:
    And, in some corner of the Hubbub coucht,
Make Game of that which makes as much of Thee.

For in and out, above, about, below,
'Tis nothing but a Magic Shadow-show,
    Play'd in a Box whose Candle is the Sun,
Round which we Phantom Figures come and go.

And if the Wine you drink, the Lip you press,
End in the Nothing all Things end in – Yes –
    Then fancy while Thou art, Thou art but what
Thou shalt be – Nothing – Thou shalt not be less.

While the Rose blows along the River Brink,
With old Khayyám and Ruby Vintage drink:
    And when the Angel with his darker Draught
Draws up to Thee – take that, and do not shrink.

'Tis all a Chequer-board of Nights and Days
Where Destiny with Men for Pieces plays:
    Hither and thither moves, and mates, and slays,
And one by one back in the Closet lays.

The Ball no Question makes of Ayes and Noes,
But Right or Left, as strikes the Player goes;
    And He that toss'd Thee down into the Field,
He knows about it all – He knows – HE knows!

The Moving Finger writes; and, having writ,
Moves on: nor all thy Piety nor Wit
    Shall lure it back to cancel half a Line,
Nor all thy Tears wash out a Word of it.

And that inverted Bowl we call The Sky,
Whereunder crawling coop't we live and die,
    Lift not thy hands to *It* for help – for It
Rolls impotently on as Thou or I.

With Earth's first Clay They did the Last Man's knead,
And then of the Last Harvest sow'd the Seed:
    Yea, the first Morning of Creation wrote
What the Last Dawn of Reckoning shall read.

I tell Thee this – When, starting from the Goal,
Over the shoulders of the flaming Foal
    Of Heav'n Parwín and Mushtarí they flung,
In my predestin'd Plot of Dust and Soul.

The Vine had struck a Fibre; which about
If clings my Being – let the Sufi flout;
    Of my Base Metal may be filed a Key,
That shall unlock the Door he howls without.

And this I know: whether the one True Light,
Kindle to Love, or Wrath – consume me quite,
　　One Glimpse of It within the Tavern caught
Better than in the Temple lost outright.

Oh, Thou, who didst with Pitfall and with Gin
Beset the Road I was to wander in,
　　Thou wilt not with Predestination round
Enmesh me, and impute my Fall to Sin?

Oh, Thou, who Man of baser Earth didst make,
And who with Eden didst devise the Snake;
　　For all the Sin wherewith the Face of Man
Is blacken'd, Man's Forgiveness give – and take!

Kúza-Náma

Listen again. One Evening at the Close
Of Ramazán, ere the better Moon arose,
　　In that old Potter's Shop I stood alone
With the clay Population round in Rows.

And, strange to tell, among that Earthen Lot
Some could articulate, while others not:
　　And suddenly one more impatient cried –
'Who *is* the Potter, pray, and who the Pot?'

Then said another – 'Surely not in vain
My Substance from the common Earth was ta'en,
　　That He who subtly wrought me into Shape
Should stamp me back to common Earth again.'

Another said – 'Why, ne'er a peevish Boy,
Would break the Bowl from which he drank in Joy;
　　Shall He that *made* the Vessel in pure Love
And Fancy, in an after Rage destroy!'

None answer'd this; but after Silence spake
A Vessel of a more ungainly Make:
  'They sneer at me for leaning all awry;
What! did the Hand then of the Potter shake?'

Said one – 'Folks of a surly Tapster tell,
And daub his Visage with the Smoke of Hell;
  They talk of some strict Testing of us – Pish!
He's a Good Fellow, and 'twill all be well.'

Then said another with a long-drawn Sigh,
'My Clay with long oblivion is gone dry:
  But, fill me with the old familiar Juice,
Methinks I might recover by-and-bye!'

So while the Vessels one by one were speaking,
One spied the little Crescent all were seeking:
  And then they jogg'd each other, 'Brother! Brother!
Hark to the Porter's Shoulder-knot a-creaking!'

Ah, with the Grape my fading Life provide,
And wash my Body whence the Life has died,
  And in a Windingsheet of Vine-leaf wrapt,
So bury me by some sweet Garden-side.

That ev'n my buried Ashes such a Snare
Of Perfume shall fling up into the Air,
  As not a True Believer passing by
But shall be overtaken unaware.

Indeed the Idols I have loved so long
Have done my Credit in Men's Eye much wrong:
  Have drown'd my Honour in a shallow Cup,
And sold my Reputation for a Song.

Indeed, indeed, Repentance oft before
I swore – but was I sober when I swore?
 And then and then came Spring, and Rose-in-hand
My threadbare Penitence apieces tore.

And much as Wine has play'd the Infidel,
And robb'd me of my Robe of Honour – well,
 I often wonder what the Vintners buy
One half so precious as the Goods they sell.

Alas, that Spring should vanish with the Rose!
That Youth's sweet-scented Manuscript should close!
 The Nightingale that in the Branches sang,
Ah, whence, and whither flown again, who knows!

Ah Love! could thou and I with Fate conspire
To grasp this sorry Scheme of Things entire,
 Would not we shatter it to bits – and then
Remould it nearer to the Heart's Desire!

Ah, Moon of my Delight who know'st no wane,
The Moon of Heav'n is rising once again:
 How oft hereafter rising shall she look
Through this same Garden after me – in vain!

And when Thyself with shining Foot shall pass
Among the Guests Star-scatter'd on the Grass,
 And in thy joyous Errand reach the Spot
Where I made one – turn down an empty Glass!

TAMÁM SHUD

Translated by EDWARD FITZGERALD

Omar Khayyam (1048–1122) was a mathematician, astronomer, poet and philosopher. Born in Nishapur, the son of a tent maker, he studied and worked in Balkh, Samarkand and Isfahan. When his master, the Seljuk Sultan Malik Shah died in 1092 he made the pilgrimage to Mecca, returning to serve as court astrologer. His quatrains, a wonderful fusion of scepticism and free thought, set amongst the pleasures of the world were translated by Edward Fitzgerald (1809–83) in 1859. They have become an essential element of English literary culture beloved by Rossetti, Swinburne, Ruskin and William Morris. This edition (the fifth) incorporates Fitzgerald's last hand-written corrections and was published posthumously in 1889.

Song of a Desert Nomad

O you who prefer the dull life of the town
to wide, free solitude,
do you despise nomadic tents
because they are light, not heavy
like houses of stone and lime?
If only you knew of the desert's secret!
But ignorance is the cause of all evil.
If you could only but awake in the dawning Sahara
and set forth on this carpet of pearls,
where flowers of all colour shower delight
and perfume on our way.
We breathe an air that lengthens life,
because it ne'er blew on the refuse of towns!
If at dawn, after the night's dew,
you would from a high point look into the distance,
you would see on the measureless horizon
fallow beasts grazing on scented meadows.
At a moment like this all care would leave thee
and rest would enter thy restless heart.
On the day of decampment the camels howdahs
are like anemones weighed down by rain.
They cover virgins, who peep out through peepholes.
Ah peephole which the eye of the houris fills!
Behind them sing the drivers in high pitch,
their song more gripping than flutes and cymbals.
But we, on noble horses
whose decorations cover breast and croup,
stir ourselves into a gallop.
We hunt gazelles and beasts of prey.

None can outrun our rapid coursing!
At night we return to the tribe
which has already encamped on an unspotted site.
The earth is like musk: even purer it is;
and generous too, moistened at dawn and dusk by rain.
There we put up our tents in rows.
The earth is dotted with them as the sky with stars.
Those who have passed on truly said
– and truth undergoeth no change –
beauty is found in two things,
in a verse and in a tent of skin.
When our camels graze at night,
their lowing resounds like the thunder of early morning.
They are the ships of the desert; whoso travels
on them is saved; but how dangerous are the ships
                                      of the sea!

They are our mehari, swift as antelopes,
through them and our horses we achieve fame.
Our horses are always saddled for battle;
who ever appeals for our aid, for him we are ready.
For fame we have sold our citizenship forever,
for fame is not won in the town!
We are kings! None can compare himself with us!
Does he then truly live, who lives in shame?

EMIR ABDEL KADER

Emir Abdel Kader, the heroic chief of the resistance of
the western tribes to the French invasion of Algeria from
1830–48, was the son of a prominent sheikh of the Sufi
Qadiriyia brotherhood. He would die an exile in Damascus,
honoured by all the peoples of the book for his conduct.

The Paladin of Qazwin

Now hear a pleasant tale – and mark the scene –
About the way and custom of Qazwin,
Where barbers ply their needles to tattoo
Folk's arms and shoulders with designs in blue.

Once a Qazwani spoke the barber fair:
'Tattoo me please; make something choice and rare.'
'What figure shall I paint, O paladin?'
'A furious lion: punch him boldly in.
Leo is my ascendant: come, tattoo
A lion, and let him have his fill of blue.'
'On what place must I prick the deft design?'
'Trace it upon my shoulder, line by line,'
He took the needle and dabbed and dabbed it in.
Feeling his shoulder smart, the paladin
Began to yell – 'You have killed me quite, I vow:
What is this pattern you are doing now?'
'Why, sir, a lion, as you ordered me.'
'Commencing with what limb?' demanded he.
'His tail,' was the reply. 'O best of men,
Leave out the tail, and start, I beg, again.
The lion's tail and rump chokes me to death;
It's stuck fast in my windpipe, stops my breath.
O lion-maker, let him have no tail,
Or under these sharp stabs my heart will fail.'
Another spot the barber 'gan tattoo,
Without fear, without favour, without rue.
'Oh, oh! Which part of him is this? Oh dear!'
'This,' said the barber, 'is your lion's ear.'

'Pray, doctor, not an ear of any sort!
Leave out his ears and cut the business short.'
The artist quickly set to work once more:
Again our hero raised a doleful roar.
'On which third limb now is the needle employed?'
'His belly, my dear sir.' 'Hold, hold!' he cried.
'Perish the lion's belly, root and branch!
How should the glutted lion want a paunch?'
Long stood the barber there in mute dismay,
His finger 'twixt his teeth, then flung away
The needle, crying, 'All the wide world o'er
Has such a thing e'er happened here heretofore?
Why, God himself did ne'er make, I tell ye,
A lion without tails or ear or belly.

MORAL

Brother, endure the pain with patience fresh,
To gain deliverance from the miscreant flesh.
Whoso is freed from selfhood's vain conceit,
Sky, sun and moon fall down to worship at his feet.

from the *Mathnawi-i-Ma'nawi* of
JELALEDDIN RUMI

Jalâl al-Dîn or Jelaleddin Rumi (meaning from Rum, or Roman
Asia Minor) or Mawlona (Our Master) is Persia's greatest mystical
poet. He is medieval Islam's greatest gift to the world. His
rapturous love poetry can be read for secular delight or as a
mystical meditation. He was born at Balkh in Afghanistan
in 1207 but journeyed through Iraq, Arabia and Syria as a child
before his father, a professor of theology, settled at Konya, capital

of the Seljuks. Jalâl al-Dîn succeeded his father as professor though the great turning point in his life was in 1244 when he met the wandering Dervish, Shams al-Din of Tabriz. He died in 1273 and so it was left to his disciple, Husam al-Din and his son, Sultan Walad, to collect and codify his vast output of couplets and fables.

My Prince and Lover was Mine Own Again

Sung by Muhabba, the estranged slave-girl concubine of Caliph Mutawakkil, on the lute and overheard by her master the night he had also dreamt of her. After which he exclaimed at the marvellous coincidence and took her by the hand and they went into her chamber.

I wander through the Palace in my sorrow,
And no one has a kindly word for me:
If I have sinned, cannot regrets appease him?
Will not some friend plead with my Lord for me?

Last night – I dreamed – and oh my dream was happy:
My prince and lover was mine own again.
Then broke the cruel dawn and found me weeping ,
– I was unhappy and alone again.

MUHABBA

The Things of the World

The things of the world from end to end are the goal of
                                desire and greed,
And I set before this heart of mine the things which I most
                                do need,
But a score of things I have chosen out of the world's
                                unnumbered throng,
That in quest of these I my soul may please and speed
                                my life along.
Verse, and song, and minstrelsy, and wine full-flavoured
                                and sweet,
Backgammon, and chess, and the hunting-ground, and the
                                falcon and cheetah fleet;
Field and ball, and audience-hall, and battle, and banquet rare,
Horse, and arms, and a generous hand, and praise of my
                                Lord and prayer.

KING QABUS, SON OF WASHMGIR,
an Emir of Tabaristan, transcribed by E. G. Browne

Lament for the Desert

When Caliph Mu'awiya overheard this lament in the marble and mosaic clad halls of his great palace in Damascus, he listened to the end and then ordered that his wife be returned back to her bedouin tribe in the Arabian desert.

A tent, where through the winds in gentle wafts should breathe
Were dearer far to me than palace high and fair;
To dress in camlet smock, with cool and placid eye,
Were fairer far to me than robes of silk to wear;
A wayward camel-colt behind the litter train
Were dearer far to me than hinny debonair;
A dog that bayed at guests as they came near
Were fairer far to me than cat with fondling air;
To eat a modest meal aside within the tent
Were dearer far to me than to feast on dainties rare;
The sighing moan of winds that blow through every wadhi
Were fairer far to me than the sound of courtly airs:
A slim but generous youth from amongst my uncle's sons
Were dearer far to me than a well-fed mount, I swear.

BY MAYSUN, WIFE OF CALIPH MU'AWIYA

MOALLÁKÁT

or the Seven Golden Odes of Pagan Arabia

Translated by LADY ANNE BLUNT
Versification by WILFRID SCAWEN BLUNT

The *Moallákát*, or *Seven Golden Odes of Pagan Arabia*, arises from an epic tradition that existed amongst the Yemenite clans that dispersed throughout the Arabian peninsula in the second century AD. These poems were probably composed some three hundred years later. Tradition has it that these *Golden Odes* or *Suspended Poems* were chosen at an annual fair held at Okád, in western Nejd, after which the elected odes were hung in the Kaaba in Mecca. The Arab kings of Híra and Ghassán would play host to these poets, since to do so improved their reputation. These doughty *Poets of the Ignorance*, as the Islamic writers call them, were their own heroes, living out epic adventures at night and sleeping by day. They were neither superstitious nor anything more than nominally religious. Their moral code was based on tribal honour, and thus courage, generosity, even philanthropy were tantamount. Hospitality and the desire for blood-revenge were the two highest virtues. The elevated status of women gave rise to a chivalric code to which Europe's own would later owe a great deal. The woman of noble blood is the primary muse in the odes but the woman once loved and then lost also receives considerable attention. Desert life meant isolation and thus unusually strong interdependence for a couple. But the tribe did convene whenever a *ráhla* or 'general move' happened, as described in Zohéyr's poem in the *Moallákát*.

The first of these 'Golden Odes', Imr el Káis, is thought to have appeared around AD 545 and the latest, namely Zohéyr's, in about AD 605, less than twenty years before the spread of Islam. It is thought that the new religion (and its formalisation) put an end to composition of this nature, although how quickly and how profoundly has been a matter of considerable debate. Certainly these hedonistic desert bards displayed a realism in their portrayals of nature and avoided artifice or mysticism at all times. Such qualities are rare in Arabian literature after the spread of Mohammed's teaching. And as Islam spread, so these tribes grew less insular and began to intermarry.

And yet it was thanks to the spread of Islam that what remained of the pre-Islamic Arabian odes were carefully recorded by schools set up for the purpose. The talent of the poets is even said to have been noticed by Mohammed himself who is rumoured to have exclaimed, on meeting Zóheyr, 'God keep me from his spirit!' One can understand his fear. This is not the poetry of a peaceful, settled people. It speaks of an existence at once wild and heroic, shocking and admirable, of a culture ruthless to foes and generous to guests and, above all, of valiant warrior-heroes galloping across the sun-baked sands of the Arabian peninsula.

The Ode of Imr El Káis

Weep, ah weep love's losing, love's with its dwelling-place
    set where the hills divide Dakhúli and Háumali.
Túdiha and Mikrat! There the hearthstones of her
stand where the South and North winds cross-weave
                        the sand-furrows.
See the white-doe droppings strewn by the wind on them,
    black on her floors forsaken, fine-grain of peppercorns.
Here it was I watched her, lading her load-camels,
    stood by these thorn-trees weeping tears as of colocynth.
Here my twin-friends waited, called to me camel-borne:
    Man! not of grief thou diest. Take thy pain patiently.
Not though tears assuage thee, deem it beseemeth thee
    Thus for mute stones to wail thee, all thy foes witnesses.
What though fortune flout thee! Thus Om Howéyrith did,
    thus did thy Om Rébabi, fooled thee in Másali.
O, where these two tented, sweet was the breath of them,
    sweet as of musk their fragrance, sweet as of garánfoli.
Mourned I for them long days, wept for the love of them,
    tears on my bosom raining, tears on my sword-handle.
Yet, was I unvanquished. Had I not happiness,
    I, at their hands in Dáret, Dáret of Jáljuli?

O that day of all days! Slew I my milch-camel,
    feasted the maidens gaily, – well did they load for me!
Piled they high the meat-strings. All day they pelted me,
    pelted themselves with fatness, fringes of camel-meat.
Climbed I to her howdah, sat with Onéyzata,
    while at my raid she chided: Man! Must I walk afoot?

Swayed the howdah wildly, she and I close in it:
    there! my beast's back is galled now. Slave of Grief,
                                    down with thee.
Answered I: Nay, sweet heart, loosen the reign of him.
    Think not to stay my kisses. Here will I harvest them.
Grieve not for thy camel. Grudge not my croup-riding.
    Give me – and thee – to taste things sweeter than
                                    clove-apples,
Kisses on thy white teeth, teeth, nay the pure petals,
    even and clean and close-set, wreathing a camomile.
Wooed have I thy equals, maidens and wedded ones.
Her, the nursling's mother, did I not win to her?
What though he wailed loudly, babe of the amulets,
    turned she not half towards him, half of her clasped to me?
Woe is me, the hard heart! How did she mock at me,
    high on the sand-hill sitting, vowing to leave and go!
Fatma, nay, my own love, though thou wouldst break with me,
    still be thou kind awhile, leave me not utterly.
Clean art thou mistaken. Love is my malady.
    Ask me the thing I choosest. Straight will I execute.
If so be thou findest ought in thy lover wrong,
    cast from thy back my garments, moult thee my finery.
Woe is me, the hard heart! When did tear's trouble thee
    save for my soul's worse wounding, stricken and near
                                    to die?

Fair too was that other, she the veil-hidden one,
    howdahed how close, how guarded! Yet did she
                                    welcome me.
Passed I twixt her tent-ropes, – what though her near-of-kin
    lay in the dark to slay me, blood-shedders all of them.
Came I at the midnight hour when the Pleiades
    showed as the links of seed-pearls binding the sky's girdle.

Stealing in, I stood there. She had cast off from her
    every robe but one robe, but her night-garment.
Tenderly she scolded: what is this stratagem?
    Speak on thine oath, thy mad one. Stark is thy lunacy.
Passed we out together while she drew after us
    on our twin track to hide it, wise, her embroideries,
Fled beyond the camp-lines. There in security
    dark in the sand we lay down far from the prying eyes.
By her plaits I wooed her, drew her face near to me,
    won to her waist how frail-lined, her of the ankle-rings.
Fair-faced she – no redness – noble of countenance,
    smooth as of glass her bosom, bare with its necklaces.
Thus are pearls yet virgin, seen through the dark water,
    clear in the sea-depths gleaming, pure, inaccessible.
Coyly she withdraws her, shows her a cheek, a lip,
    she a gazelle of Wújra, – yearling the fawn with her.
Roe-like her throat slender, white as an áriel's,
    sleek to thy lips up-lifted, – pearls are its ornament.
On her shoulders fallen thick lie the locks of her,
    dark as the dark date-clusters hung from the
                          palm-branches.
See the side-plaits pendent, high on the brows of her,
    tressed in a knot, the caught ones fast with the fallen ones.
Slim her waist, – a well-cord scarce has its slenderness.
    Smooth are her legs as reed-stems, stripped at a
                        water-head.
The morn through she sleepeth, musk-strewn in indolence,
    hardly at noon hath risen, girded her day dresses.
Soft her touch, – her fingers fluted as water-worms,
    sleek as the snakes of Thóyba, tooth-sticks at Ishali.
Lighteneth she night's darkness, ay, as an evening lamp
    hung for a sign of guidance lone on a hermitage.

Who but shall desire her, seeing her standing thus,
  Half in her childhood's short frock, half in her
                                woman's robe!
Strip thee of youth's fooling, thou in thy manhood's prime.
  Yet to her love be faithful, – hold it a robe to thee.
Many tongues have spoken, warned me of craft in love.
  Yet have they failed an answer, – all were thine enemies.

Dim the drear-night broodeth, – veil upon veil let down,
  dark as a mad sea raging, tempting the heart of me.
Spake I to night stoutly while he, a slow camel,
  dragged with his hind-feet halting, – gone the
                                forehand of him.
Night, I cried, thou snail night, when wilt thou turn to day?
When? Though in sooth day's dawning worse were
                                than thou to me.
Sluggard Night, what stays thee? Chained hang the
                                stars of thee
  fast to the rocks with hempen ropes set unmoveable.

Water-skins with some folk – ay, with the thong of them
  laid on my nága's wither – borne have I joyfully,
Crossed how lone the rain-ways, bare as an ass-belly;
  near me the wolf, starved gamester, howled to his progeny.
Cried I: Wolf, thou wailest. Surely these lives of ours,
  thine and my own, go empty, robbed of prosperity.
All we won we leave here. Whoso shall follow us,
  seed in our corn-track casting, reap shall he barrenness.

Rode I forth at day-dawn, – birds in their nests asleep –
  stout on my steed, the sleek-coat, him the game-vanquisher.
Lo, he chargeth, turneth, – gone is he – all in one,
  like to a rock stream-trundled, hurled from its eminence.

Red-bay he, – his loincloth chafing the ribs of him
   Shifts as a rain-stream smoothing stones in a riverbed.
Hard is he, – he snorteth loud in the pride of him,
   fierce as a full pot boiling, bubbling beneath the lid.
Straineth he how stoutly, while, as spent fishes swim,
   tied to his tracks the fleet ones plough his steps wearily.
See, in scorn he casteth youth from the back of him,
   leaveth the horseman cloakless, naked the hard-rider.
As a sling-stone hand-whirled, so is the might of him,
   loosed from the string that held it, hurled from
                 the spliced ribbon.
Lean his flanks, gazelle-like, legs as the ostrich's;
   he like a strong wolf trotteth, lithe as a fox-cub he.
Stout his frame; behind him, look, you shall note of him
   full-filled the hind-leg gap, tail with no twist in it.
Polished, hard his quarters, smooth as the pounding-stone
   used for a bridegroom's spices, grind-slab of colocynth.
As the henna juice lies died on beard grown hoar,
   so on his neck the bloodstains mark the game
                     down-ridden.
Rushed we on the roe-herd. Sudden, as maids at play
   circling in skirts low-trailing, forth leaped the does of it.
Flashing fled they, jewels, shells set alternately
   on a young gallant's neck-string, hits the high pedigreed.
Yet he gained their leaders, far while behind him lay
   bunched in a knot the hindmost, ere they fled scatterwise.
'Twixt the cow and bull herds held he in wrath his road;
   made he of both his booty, – sweatless the neck of him.
All that day we roasted, seethed the sweet meat of them,
   row upon row in cauldrons, firelighters all of us.
Nathless home at nightfall, he in the forefront still.
   Where is the eye shall bind him? How shall it follow him?

The night through he watcheth, scorneth him down to lay,
  close, while I sleep, still saddled, bridled by side of me.

Friend, thou seest the lightning. Mark where it wavereth,
  gleameth like fingers twisted, clasped in the cloud rivers.
Like a lamp new-lighted, so is the flash of it,
  trimmed by a hermit nightly pouring oil-sésame.
Stood I long a watcher, twin-friends how dear with me,
  till in Othéyb it faded, ended in Dáriji.
By its path we judged it: rain over Káttan is;
  far in Sítar it falleth, streameth in Yáthboli.
Gathereth gross the flood-head damned in Kutéyfati.
  Woe to the trees, the branched ones! Woe the kanáhboli!
El Kanáan hath known it, quailed from the lash of it.
  Down from their lairs it driveth hot-foot the ibexes.
Known it too hath Téyma; standeth no palm of her
  there, nor no house low-founded, – none but her
                                        rock-buildings.
Stricken stood Thabíra whelmed by the rush of it,
  like an old chief robe-folded, bowed in his striped mantle.
Nay, but he Mujéymir, tall-peaked at dawn of day,
  showed like a spinster's distaff tossed on the flood-water.
Cloud-wrecked lay the valley piled with the load of it,
  high as in sacks the Yemámi heapeth his corn-measures.
Seemed it then the songbirds, wine-drunk at sun-rising,
  loud through the valleys shouted, maddened with spiceries,
While the wild-beast corpses, grouped like great bulbs up-torn
  cumbered the hollow places, drowned in the night-trouble.

Imr-el-Kais, a tribal prince from the Yemen, was murdered by
officers of the Byzantine Emperor in AD 565, in the forty-fifth
year of his adventurous, passionate life.

The Ode of Tárafa

The tent lines these of Kháula in stone-stricken Tháhmadi.
  See where the fire has touched them, dyed dark as the
                                              hands of her.
'Twas here thy friends consoled thee that day with
                                              thee comforting,
  cried; not of grief, thou faint-heart! Men die not thus easily.
Aye, here the howdahs passed thee at day-dawn, how royally!
  stood for the Dédi pastures; – a white fleet they seemed
                                              to thee,
Ships tall-rigged from Adáuli – of Yámin the build of them –
  wandering wide the night through, to meet at the sun-rising.
Thus climbed the long wave-lines, their prows set how loftily!
  ploughing the drifted ridges, sand heaped by the sand-seers.

Alas for the dark-lipped one, the maid of the topazes,
  hardly yet grown a woman, sweet fruit-picking loiterer!
A girl, a fawn still fawnless, which browses the thorn-bushes,
close to the doe-herd feeding, aloof in the long valleys.
I see her mouth-slit smiling, her teeth, – nay, a camomile
  White on the white sand blooming and moist with the
                                              night-showers.
Sun-steeped it is, pure argent, white all but the lips of her,
  these are too darkly painted to shrink from the sun-burning.
The face of her how joyous, the day's robe enfolding her,
  clean as a thing fresh-fashioned, untouched by sad time-fingers.

Enough! New joys now claim me. Ay, mount and away from her!
  Here on my swift-foot camel I laugh at love's bitterness.
Ship-string is she, my naga, my stout-timbered road-goer,
  footing the long-lined pathway – a striped cloak – in front of us.

103

Steel tempered are her sinews. She runs like an ostrich-hen,
  one which has fled defying the ash-plumed proud lord of her.
Out-paces she the best-born, shank still on shank following
  threading the mazes lightly. Ah, what foot shall follow her?
The spring-long on Kufféyn she has wandered, her kind with her,
  pastured in pleasant places, the rain-watered thyme-valleys,
Has turned to her herds calling, aloft in wrath brandishing,
  scared by the thick-furred red thief, that proud tuft the tail
                                                      of her.
Her tail sways this way and that way – a falcon the wings of him
  bating her flanks impatient – erect stands the bone of it –
So lasheth she in anger anon her croup-rider's knee,
  then her own shrunken udder, a drought-withered water-skin.
Note well her limbs perfection, her thighs like the elbow-worn
  jambs of a city gateway, two smooth shafts of porphyry.
Her barrel – a stone well-mouth, like bent bones the curves of it,
  cave where the neck-shaft enters, ends in an arched hollow.
Deep dens are her two armpits, a tree with cavities.
  Bows are her rib-bones bended, her spine the hands
                                              holding them.
Her elbows are twin-buckets, the pails of a water-man
  wide-set, the neck between them the strong man who
                                              carries them.
Bridge-like and Roman-built. How swore he its architect!
  none should leave work or loiter, its keystone unlaid by them.
Red chestnut is her chin-tuft, a vast vault the back of her.
  Swift-step her hind feet follow the path of her fore-footing.
Her legs are a cord twisted. Towards the arms of her
  slant from the shoulders outward, a tent-roof the slope of them.
So sways she, the strong-skulled one, and lightly her
                                              shoulder blades
  rise with her spine alternate, a rhyme with the march of her.

Like rain-pools in the smooth-rock, so, flecking the sides of her,
  white stand the girth-marks, witness once of the sores on them.
Her neck, how tall, how proud-set! Behold her! She raises it
  high as in ships of Díjleh the point of a stern-rudder.
Her head-piece a stout anvil, and, joined to it hardily
  sharp as a file the neck-ridge, fixed as a vice to it.
Her jowl a Syrian parchment, clean vellum the lip of her
  smooth as a hide of Yémen, no skin-crease nor fold in it.
Her eyes two mirrors shining, her bent brows the shade of them,
  pitted with deep-set hollows, as rock-holes for rainwater.
Eyes dark-rimmed, pure of dust-stains. You gaze in the depths
                                                      of them
    as in a wild cow's wild eyes, scared for the calf of her.
Ears fearful of the night-sounds, the whispers, the murmurings
  caught in the darkness passing – night – day they can
                                                never rest never.
Their thorn-tips tell her lineage, a wild bull's of Háumala
  raging alone forsaken; her breeding you read in them.
Heart watchful of strange dangers, yet stout in the face of them.
  Firm as a test-stone standing where cleft lie the base-pebbles.
Lip slit, nose pierced for nose-ring, how slender its cartilage!
  Nobly she lowers it running and stretched to the front of her.
I strike at her my nága: I force her: I hurry her,
  while in our path the false-lights lure us to follow them.
The gait of her how rhythmic! She sways like a dancing-girl,
  one with the white skirts trailing, who bends to the lord of her.
Obedient to your riding, she slackens your outrunning,
  watches the hide-thong twisted, the speed that you need of her.
Her head by your hand close held, your knee-crutch how
                                                near to it!
    Then with her fore arms swimming, an ostrich, she flies
                                                with you

Thus rode I, and thus spake he, the friend of my tear-sheddings:
    O for the wit to cure thee, but and my own sorrows!
His soul within him trembled; it seemed to his hardihood
    death and a sure destruction, though far we from road-farers.
For which of us is valiant? When men speak of true valour,
    I feel my own the name named. Straight am I roused by it.
No recreant I, my tent-ridge I hide from no enemy.
    Nor in the far hills build it who bring men a swift succour.
The hand that seeks shall find me. I stand at the gatherings.
    Ay, where men tap the wineskin, 'tis there they shall
                           speak with me.
What day the tribes assemble, behold me conspicuous,
    sitting as fits my lineage, nor go I in fear of them.
Beside me my companions, bright stars of nobility.
    Dyed is her robe of saffron the girl who pours out for us.
O sweet is her shirt's neck-slit, set wide to the eyes of us.
    Soft is the thing it hides there. We bade her: Now, sing to us.
Ay sing to us: we prayed her. And she, with monotony
    striking a low note slowly chaunted unchangingly.
O strange it was that cadence: it came back the wail of it,
    grave as a mother's grieving the one son new-slain from her.

Thus sang she. And I spared not the full cups of revelry,
    not till my spoil was wasted, my whole wealth's inheritance.
Then left they that loved me. They shunned me my tribe-fellows.
    Sat I alone forsaken, a mange-stricken male camel.
Nathless the poor showed pity, the sons of Earth's particles,
    these and the alien tent-lords, the far chiefs befriended me.
You only did revile me. Yet, say, ye philosophers,
    was that same wealth eternal I squandered in feasting you?
Could all you my fate hinder? Friends, run we ahead of it,
    rather our lives enjoying, since Time will not wait for us.

And, truly, but for three things in youth's day of vanity,
    fain would I see them round me the friends at my
                              death-bedding,
As first: to outstrip the sour ones, be first at the winebibbing,
    ay, at the blink of day-dawn when mixed the cup foams for me;
And next, to ride their champion, who none have to succour them,
    fierce on my steed, the led one, a wolf roused and
                              thirst-stricken;
And third, to lie the day-long, while wild clouds are wildering,
    close in her tent of goat's hair, the dearest beloved of me.
O noble she, a tree-stem unpruned in her maidenhood,
    tall as a branch of Kírwa, where men hang their ornaments.
'Tis thus I slake my soul's rage, the life-thirst so wild in me.
    If we died tomorrow, think, which would go thirstier?
For lo, his grave the miser's! Lo, next to it the prodigal's!
    Both are alike, scant favour to hoarder or squanderer.
'Neath mounds of earth the twain lie, a low stone atop of them,
    heavy and broad and shapeless, with new slabe o'erlaying it.
Death is no subtle chooser. He takes all, the free-chooser,
    ay, and the rogues close-fisted, the fast-handed gold-hiders.
And life's heap lies unguarded. The night-thieves make spoil of it.
    All that these leave the day-thieves straight way come
                              plundering.
Nay, by the life – I swear it, though fast fly the heels of him,
    Death has a lead-rope round him, loose though it seem to you.

Ha! How is this? My kinsman? My fool-cousin Máleki?
    Daily, as I draw near him, he turns his mad back on me.
He frowns I know not wherefore. He flouts me, as once with them
    Kurt, in the face of all men, flouted and jibed at me.
His help he has denied me; and truly, our brotherhood
    tried in the fire of asking lies dead in love's sepulchre.

My word his words discredit. Yet all I for Mábadi
    asked was a poor assistance to gather his lost camels,
I who hold fast to kinship. I swear by the luck of thee,
    when they shall want hard riding, that day they shall
                                                    fawn on me.
What day their tribes need succour, when loudly their
                                                    womenfolk
    cry from his hand the oppressor's to hands that are mightier.
Be but their honour tainted, I straight will pour out for them
    death as from brimming cisterns, nor ask for an argument.
They rail at and revile me, who know no ill-doer;
    me, who have borne their burdens, cast would they out
                                                    from them.
Yet, had my friend been other, this Málek of larger soul,
    long had my pain been ended, a respiting found for me.
Shame on him for his baseness. His black hand would
                                                    strangle me,
    whether I thanked or sued him, or turned but my back on him.
O cruel is the sword-stroke: it bites with an Indian edge:
    yet is their temper keener, the clowns I call kin to me.
Then leave me to my own ways, my tent set in Dárghadi,
    far from the eyes of all men, and earn thee my gratitude.
Had he, the Lord, so willed it, my name had been Kháladi,
    or had he willed it Amer, or Káis, or Marthádi.
Wealth had been mine and increase, ay, all that men most covet,
    sons as a gift of heaven, a proud-lined posterity.
Yet see me a man subtle, one lithe-souled and lithe-bodied,
    quick as a snake for wounding, whose head is a hurt for them.
The oath my tongue has sworn to is this, to keep close to me
    ever my sword-blade loosened; of Indies the edge of it.
Such blade, if I take vengeance and rise up and smite with it,
    needs not a second down-stroke; I wield me no wood-chopper.

My sword is my true-brother. It grudges no blood-spilling.
    Called on to spare, it answers: My lord alone holdeth me.
Thus was I when men armed them and rushed to the battlefield:
    grasped I my sword-hilt foremost, nor feared what
                                        fate doomed for me.

Herds knelt, their necks stretched earth-long. How scare
                                        them the eyes of me,
    me with my sword drawn marching, its sheath cast away
                                        from me.
There passed a strong-fared nága, a full-uddered milch-camel,
    joy of her lord, the gray-beard, a hot man, though time-troubled.
He shouted when she fell there, her stout sinews houghed by me:
    Man, art thou blind who seest not thy sword hath
                                        done robbery?
He spake, and to his friends turned: Behold him, this wine-bibber!
    What is his rage against us, his wild words, his drink-folly?
Yet paused: Nay, give him wide room and leave it to profit him:
    herd we the scared ones together, lest more he should slay
                                        of them.
Then fell the maids aroasting its fair flesh the foal of her,
    nor of the fat denied us, the whole hump our prize of it.
We cast the arrows gaily, the dun-shafts, the fire-hardened:
    each time the holder held them, straight way I won with them.

When I am dead, speak kindly, thou daughter of Mábadi:
    rend for thy sake thy garments as one worth the love of thee.
Nor count me with the lewd folk, the night-knaves, the
                                        roysterers,
    men with nor wit nor wisdom nor will to do weightily,
Men slow to deeds of virtue, men swift but in ill-doing,
    men by the brave held lightly, with spread palms and
                                        brow-knitting.

For, had I been a weakling, know well, their mad hate of me
  long had been my destruction, their blind wrath my butchery.
Only it wards me from them the fear of my hand's valour,
  this, and my faith untainted, my fame too of ancestry.
Once on a time I bound me with vows, on the battlefield
  ever to guard the weak posts, points where the foe threatened,
Points where the bravest faltered, where pale men stood
                                            panic-struck'
  where they the strong-hearts trembled, faint through the
                                            fear of them.
Nay, by thy life, I fear not. I hold not time weariness;
  neither hath day distressed me, nor night what it brought to me.
Because I see death spares none. It smites with an even hand,
  bows not to names exalted, nor knows it men's dignities;
Because with death behind me, my flight can avail me not,
  neither can I outwit him, he lying in wait for me.
Because if one be proved vain by those who seek aid of him,
  helpless to hurt the harmful, better he perished.
The days to come, what are they? A handful, a borrowing:
  vain is the thing thou fearest. Today is the life of thee.
And death is a well-spring; to it men pass and pass:
  near them is each tomorrow; near them was yesterday.
Only shall Age, the slow-foot, arraign thee of ignorance:
  only shall One bring tidings, when least thou desirest him,
One who is hard to deal with, of whom thou art ransomer
  neither for pay nor raiment, nor madest thou tryst with him.

Tárafa was of the tribe of Dhobya, a wild bedouin youth,
imaginative, impulsive, perverse, hot-tongued and violent-
handed. He died aged twenty-six by order of the king of Hira.

The Ode of Zohéyr

Woe is me for 'Ommi' Aufa! woe for the tents of her
    lost on thy stony plain, Durráj, on thine, Mutethéllemi!
In Rákmatéyn I found our dwelling, faint lines how desolate,
    tent-marks traced like the vein-tracings blue on the wrists
                                                    of her.
Large-eyed there the wild-kine pastured, white roes how fearlessly,
    leaped, their fawns beside them, startled – I in the midst
                                                    of them.
Twenty years abroad I wander. Lo, here I stand today,
    hardly know the remembered places, seek I how painfully.
Here our hearthstones stand, ay, blackened still with
                                                    her cooking-pots,
    here our tent-trench squarely graven, grooved here our
                                                    camel-trough.
Love, when my eyes behold thy dwelling, to it I call aloud:
    Blessed be thou, O house of pleasure, greeting and joy to thee!

Friend of my soul! Dost thou behold them? Say, are
                                            there maidens there,
    camel-borne, high in their howdahs, over the Júrthum spring?
Say, are their curtains lined with scarlet, sanguine embroideries,
    veiling them from the eyes of all men, rose-tinted coverings?
Slantwise up El-Subáan they mounted – high-set the pass of it.
    With them the newborn morning's beauty, fair-face
                                                    and fortunate.
At the blink of dawn they rose and laded. Now, ere the sun is up,
    point they far to Wády Ras, straight as hand points to mouth.
Joy! Sweet joy of joys! Fair visions, human in tenderness,
    dear to the human eye that truly sees them and understands.

As the scarlet fringe of fénna seed-pops no lip hath browsed upon,
   so is the dye of their scarlet wool new-fringing the
                                   camping grounds.
And they came to the watering pool in the red rocks –
                        blue-black the depths of it.
  And they planted the tent-poles, straight and fairly, firm
                            for a dwelling-place.
They have left Kanáan on the far right hand – dark-crowned
                          the crest of it.
  How many foes in El Kanáan! And friends too, ah, how many!
But they came to El Subáan in their might, impetuous, beautiful,
   they in their howdahs of scarlet wool. O friend,
                       dost thou look on them?

I have sworn by the most illustrious dwelling, shrine
                       of processioners,
  house revered of Koréysh and Júrham, founded in piety.
I have sworn my praise to the two chieftains, men of
                       what hardihood'
  prompt to do when need shall call them, light deeds
                      and doughty deeds.
Strove ye well, ye Lords of Mórra, what though the clans of you
   long had drowned in blood their friendship, drowned
                       it in war-clamours.
Ye with Abs and Dóbían that day ye persuaded them,
   spite of feud and their death-dealing perfumes of mínshami.
For thus ye spake: Let peace be garnered, all the fair wealth of it,
   based on pay and fair exchanges, ours to establish it.
Theirs the peace and yours the glory, high names and dignities,
   you the noble twain prevailing, purging the rage of them.
Lo, in Maád ye stand exalted, ye the high-guided ones.
   He who a booty brings of glory, shall he not share in it?

Healing of wounds you dealed in hundreds, hundreds of
                                        debt-camels,
Tribe and tribe, you paid the ransom, what though the
                                        hands of you
   clean were of blood and the red shedding, ay, the least cup of it.
Yet ye brought the payment bravely, all your fair heritage,
   camels yours by right of plunder, these and your
                                        earmarked ones.

Ho! to the oath-bound tribes a greeting: Have ye not sworn to it?
   Ay, and to Dóbián a message: Will you not keep the peace?
For you may not hide from God your dealings, what though
                                        in secrecy
   deep in your heart of hearts you seal it. Nathless He knoweth it.
Knoweth and taketh note in patience, sure of His reckoning
   till the day of the great counting, waiteth or hasteneth.
War! Ye have learned it all, its teachings, well have ye tasted them.
   These are no tales that I tell you. Each is a certainty.
A smouldering coal you flung it lightly, blindly despising it.
   Lo, into raging flame it leapeth, wind-lit, destroyeth you.
Ye are ground as corn by Hate's ill-grinding, flat on her
                                        grinding-skin.
   Nay, a too fruitful camel she. Twins hath she borne to you,
Sinister sons of fear and anger, milk-fed on bitterness;
   dark as his, Aád's, their nursing. Lo, she is weaned of them.
And her hand is large to rain you harvests, evil the wealth of them.
   No such plenty Irák hath garnered, hell-grain and hate-money.

Ay, by my life, the kin was noble. Yet did it fare with them
   ill when they the peace-terms flouted. Démden's the sin of it,
His, Huséyn's, who held his counsel, hiding the thought in him,
   yielding naught and naught revealing, steeled in
                                        his stubbornness.

For he thought: My end will I accomplish. No ill shall come to me,
    fenced and armed, with might behind me, warriors, horse-riders.
Proud he stood, nor feared the tent-lords, what though

                             Om-Káshami
    watched them near, the vulture-mother, eyeing the multitude.
Strode he forth, full-armed, a wild beast, fierce for the

                             blood-letting,
    mane and claws unclipped, a lion. Who shall his anger brave?
Fearless, one who doth his vengeance swift on his wrong-doer,
    one who unassailed yet rendeth, he the first injurer.
And they pastured there their fair milch-camels, drove to

                             the waterings,
    drank of the full pools brimming over, gall in the hearts of them.
This side and that by blood divided, rank hate the meat of them,
    poison-grass to their herds hurting, mired in blood-bitterness.
Yet, by thy life, not these the guilty. Clean was the steel of them,
    pure of blood, Nahík's. They slew not him nor Muthéllemi,
Shareless sharers of the death-due. No blood of Náufali
    stood to their account, nor Wahab's, nay, nor Mukházzemi's.
Blameless! Clean! Yet have I seen them drive to the ransoming
    camel-herds untouched, unblemished, fresh from rock-valleys.
Succour to the tribe that succoured! Who but shall haste to them
    in their night of fear, of blackness! All men shall speed to them,
Since they gave, since them the avenger gained not to ill-willing,
    nay, nor suppliant failed of favour. Him they abandoned not.

I am weary of life who bear its burden fourscore and how many
    years of glory and grief counted. Well may he weary be,
I know today, the day before it, ay, and the days that were,
    yet of tomorrow I know nothing. Blind are the eyes of me.
I have seen fate strike out in the darkness, strike like a

                             blind camel:
    some it touched died straight, some lingered on to decrepitude.

I have learned that he who giveth nothing, deaf to his
                                        friends' begging,
    loosed shall be to the world's tooth-strokes: fools feet
                                        shall tread on him;
That he that doeth for his name's sake fair deeds shall further it,
    but he that of men's praise is careless dwindleth in dignity;
That he, the Lord of wealth, who spendeth nought of his
                                        heaped money,
    him his kinsfolk shall hold lightly: children shall mouth at him;
That he who keepeth faith shall find faith; who in simplicity
    shall pursue the ways accustomed, no chin shall wag at him;
That he who flieth his fate shall meet it, not, though a sky-ladder
    he shall climb, shall his fear fend him: dark death shall
                                        noose him down;
That he who gifteth the unworthy, spendthrift through idleness,
    praised shall be to his dispraising, shamed at his fool-doing;
That he, who shall refuse the lance-butts borne by the
                                        peace-bearers,
    him the lance-heads shall find fenceless, naked the flesh of him;
That he who guardeth not his tent-floor, with the whole might
                                        of him,
    cold shall be his hearthstone broken, ay, though he smote
                                        at none;
That he who flieth his kin shall fare far, foes for his guest-fellows;
    that he who his own face befouleth none else shall honour him;
That he, who casteth not the burdens laid on the back of him,
    sheer disgrace shall be his portion, waged as he merited;
That whatso a man hath by nature, wit-wealth or vanity,
    hidden deep, the day shall prove it: all shall be manifest.
For how many sat wise while silent, yet was their foolishness
    proved when their too much, too little, slid through
                                        their mouth-slitting.

The tongue is the strong man's half; the other half is the
                                        heart of him:
  all the rest is a brute semblance, rank corporality.
Truly, folly in the old is grievous; no cure is known for it:
  yet may the young their soul's unwisdom win to new sanity.

We asked once, and you gave a guerdon, – twice and again
                                        you gave:
  only the mouth that hath no silence endeth in emptiness.

It is said that Zohéyr lived to extreme age, and that aged ninety
he was brought into the Prophet's presence, and was recognised
by him as the greatest of the poets.

  The Caliph Omar called him the 'poet of poets' and even in
the days of Ignorance a 'man of piety'.

The Ode of Lebíd

Gone are they the lost camps, light flittings, long sojournings
   in Mína, in Gháula, Rijám how desolate.
Lost are they. Rayyán lies lorn, with its white torrent beds,
   scored in lines like writings left by the flood-water.
Tent-floors smooth, forsaken, bare of all that dwelt in them,
   years how long, the war-months, months too of
                             peace-pleasures.
Spots made sweet with Spring rains fresh-filled from the Zodiac,
   showers from clouds down-shaken, wind-wracks and
                             thunderclouds;
Clouds how wild of night-time, clouds of the dawn darkening,
   clouds of the red sunset, – all the speak the name of her.

Here, in green thorn-thickets, does bring forth how fearlessly;
   here the ostrich-troops come, here too the antelopes.
Wild cows, with their wild calf-sucklings standing over them,
   while their weanlings wander wide in the bare valleys.
Clean-swept lie their hearthstones, white as a new manuscript
   writ with texts fresh-graven, penned by the cataracts,
Scored with lines and circles, limned with rings and blazonings,
   as one paints a maid's cheek, point-lined in indigo.
All amazed I stood there. How should I make questionings?
   Dumb the rocks around me, silent the precipice,
Voices lost, where these dwelt who at dawn abandoning
   tent and thorn-bush fencing fled to the wilderness.
Now thy sad heart acheth, grieveth loud remembering
   girls how closely howdahed, awned with what canopies.
Every howdah curtained, lined with gauze embroideries,
   figured with festoons hung red from the pole of it.

Trooped they there the maid-folk, wild white cows of Túdiha,
    ay, or does of Wújra, long-necked, their fawns with them,
Fled as the mirage flees, fills the vale of Bíshata,
    fills the tree-clad wádies, íthel and rock-mazes.

What of her, Nowára, thy lost love, who fled from thee,
    every heart-link sundered, close loop and free fetter!
Hers the Mórra camp-fires lit how far in Fáïda,
    in Hejáz what marches! How shalt thou win to her?
Eastward move they marching, to Muhájjer wandering
    camped in Tái, in Férda, ay, in Rukhám of it.
Southward on to Yémen, to Sowéyk their sojournings,
    to Wahák el Káhri, ay, and Tilkhám of it.
Man, have done! forget her, – one too far to comfort thee!
    Who would his love garner first let him sunder it.
Shed the love that fails thee. Strong be thou, and break with her.
    Keep thy gifts for friendship, freed from thy wilderment.
Mount thee on thy nága. Travel-trained and hard she is,
    low her back with leanness, lessened the hump of her;
Shrunk her side and wasted, jaded with long journeyings,
    spare as her hide shoe-straps frayed by her road-faring.
Light she to her halter, to thy hand that guideth her,
    as a red cloud southwards loosed from its rain-burden.
Nay a fair wild-ass she; at her side the white-flanked one,
    he the scarred ass-stallion, bitten and struck for her.
Climbed they two the hilltop, he the bite-scarred ass-tyrant
    her new mood resenting, being in foal to him.
On the crags high posted watcheth he from Thálabut
    all the plains to guard her, ambushes laid for her.
Six months of Jumáda wandered have they waterless,
    browsing the moist herbage, he her high sentinel.
Till returned their thirsting, need of the far water clefts,
    all their will to win there speeding them waterwards.

What though with heels wounded, still the hot wind driveth them,
    as a furnace burning, fire-scorched the breath of it.
In their trail like a dust-cloud, like a smoke it wavereth,
    like a fire new-lighted, kindling the flame of it,
Flame fanned by the North-wind, green wood mixed with dry fuel,
    smoke aloft high curling. So is the dust of them.
He, when her pace slackened, pushed her still in front of him.
    Nay, she might not falter, tyrant he urged her on,
Till they reached the streamlet, plunged and slaked their
                                            thirst in it,
    A spring running over, crest-high the reeds of it;
All its banks a cane-brake, thick with stems o'ershadowing;
    bent are some, some standing, night-deep the shade of them.

Say is this her likeness? Or a wild cow wolf-raided
    of her sweet calf loitering, she is the van of them.
She, the short-nosed, missed it. Lows she now unendingly,
    roams the rocks, the sand-drifts, mourning and bellowing,
Lows in rage beholding that white shape, the limbs of it,
    dragged by the grey wolf-cubs, – who shall their hunger stay?
Theirs the chance to seize it, hers the short forgetfulness.
    Death is no mean archer. Mark how his arrows hit.
Stopped she then at nightfall, while the rain in long furrows
    scored the bush-grown hill-slopes, ceaseless the drip of it,
Dripped on her dark back-line, poured abroad abundantly:
    not a star the heaven showed, cloud-hung the pall of it;
One tree all her shelter, standing broad-branched, separate
    at the sand-hills edge-line, steep-set the sides of them.
She, the white cow, shone there through the dark night luminous,
    like a pearl of deep-seas, freed from the string of it.
Thus till morn, till day-dawn folded back night's canopy;
    then she fled bewildered, sliding the feet of her,

Fled through the rain lakelets, to the pool Suwáyada,
    all a seven nights' fasting twinned with the days of them,
Till despaired she wholly, till her udder milk-stricken
    shrank, so full to feed him, suckling or weaning him.
Voices now she hears near, human tones, they startle her,
    though to her eye nought is: Man! he, the bane of her!
Seeketh a safe issue, the forenoon through listening,
    now in front, behind now, fearing her enemy.
And they failed, the archers. Loosed they then to deal with her
    fine-trained hounds, the lop-eared, slender the sides of them.
These outran her lightly. Turned she swift her horns on them,
    like twin spears of Sámhar, sharp-set the points of them.
Well she knew her danger, knew if her fence failed with them
    hers must be the red death. Hence her wrath's strategy.
And she slew Kasábi, foremost hound of all of them,
    stretched the brach in blood there, ay, and Súkham of them.
Thus she is, my nága. When at noon the plains quiver
    and the hills dance sun-steeped, cloaked in the heat-tremors,
Ride I and my deeds do, nor forbear from wantoning,
    lest the fools should shame me, blame me the fault-finders.

Do not thou misprize me, thou Nowára. One am I
    binder of all love-knots, ay, and love's sunderer;
One who when love fails him, wails not long but flies from it;
    one whom one alone holds, hard death the hinderer.
What dost thou of mirth know, glorious nights, ah, how many –
    cold nor heat might mar them – spent in good company?
Came I thus discoursing to his sign, the wine-seller's
    drank at the flag-hoisting, drank till the wine grew dear,
Bidding up each full skin, – black with age the brand of it,
    pouring forth the tarred jars, breaking the seals of them;
Pure deep draughts of morning, while she played, the sweet singer
    fingering the lute-strings, showing her skill to me.

Ere the cock had crowed once, a first cup was quaffed by me:
  ere slow man had stretched him, gone was the second cup.
On what dawns sharp-winded clothed have I the cold with it,
  dawns that held the North-wind reined in the hands of them.
Well have I my tribe served, brought them aid and armament,
  slept, my mare's reins round me, nightlong their sentinel;
Ridden forth at day-dawn, climbed the high-heaped sand-ridges
  hard by the foe's marches, dun-red the slopes of them;
Watched till the red sun dipped hand-like in obscurity,
  till the night lay curtained, shrouding our weaknesses;
And I came down riding, my mare's neck held loftily
  as a palm fruit-laden, – woe to the gatherer!
Swift was she, an ostrich; galloped she how wrathfully,
  from her sides the sweat streamed, lightening the ribs of her;
Strained on her saddle; dripped with wet the neck of her,
  the white foam-flakes wreathing, edging the girth of her;
Thrusteth her neck forward, shaking her reins galloping;
  flieth as the doves fly bound for the water-springs.

At the King's Court strangers thronged from what far provinces,
  each athirst for bounty, fearing indignity.
Stiff-necked they as lions in their hate, the pride of them,
  came with stubborn, proud feet, Jinns of the wilderness.
Stopped I their vain boastings, took no ill-tongued words from them,
  let them not take licence. What were their chiefs to me?
I it was provided camels for their slaughtering,
  I who their shares portioned, drawing the lots for them.
Every mouth I feasted. Barren mount and milch-camel
  slew I for all daily. All shared the meat of them.
Far guest and near neighbour, every man rose satisfied,
  full as in Tebála, fed as in green valleys.
Ay, the poor my tent filled, thin poor souls like sick-camels,
  nágas at a tomb tied, barebacked, no shirt on them.

Loud the winter winds howled; piled we the meat dishes;
  flowed the streams of fatness, feeding the fatherless.
Thus the tribes were trysted; nor failed we the provident
  to name one, a wise man, fair-tongued, as judge for them,
One who the spoil portioned, gave to each his just measure,
  spake to all unfearing, gave or refused to give,
A just judge, a tribe-sheykh, wise, fair-worded, bountiful,
  sweet of face to all men, feared by the warriors.

Noble we; our fathers wielded power bequeathed to them,
  dealt law to the nations, each tribe its lawgiver.
All our lineage faultless, no light words our promises;
  not for us the vain thoughts, passions of common men.
Thou fool foe, take warning, whatso the Lord portioneth
  hold it a gift granted, dealt thee in equity.
Loyalty our gift was, faith unstained our heritage;
  these fair things He gave us, He the distributor.
For us a mansion built he, brave the height of it,
  lodged therein our old men, ay, and the youths of us,
All that bore our burdens, all in our tribe's sore sorrow,
  all that were our horsemen, all our high councillors.
Like the spring are these men, joy to them that wait on them,
  to the weak, the widows, towers in adversity.
Thus our kin stands faith-firm, purged of tribe-malingerers.
  Woe be to all false friends! woe to the envious!

Lebid ibn Nabia was of the tribe of the Beni Kelab. A true
bedouin who lived long enough to profess Islam and to die
during the reign of Caliph Muáwiya.

The Ode of Ántara

How many singers before me! Are there yet songs unsung?
  Dost thou, my sad soul, remember where was her
                                           dwelling place?
Tents in Jiwá, the far wádi, speak ye to me of her,
  Fair house of 'Abla my true love, blessing and joy to thee!
Doubting I paused in the pastures, seeking her camel-tracks,
  high on my swift-trotting nága tall as a citadel,
Weaving a dream of the past days, days when she dwelt in them,
  'Abla my true love, in Házzen, Summán, Mutathéllemi,
There on the sand lay the hearth-stones, black in their emptiness,
  desolate more for the loved ones fled with Om Héythami,
Fled to the land of the lions, roarers importunate.
  Daily my quest of thee darkens, daughter of Mákhrami.

Truly at first sight I loved her, I who had slain her kin,
  ay, by the life of thy father, not in inconstancy.
Love, thou hast taken possession. Deem it not otherwise.
  Thou in my heart art the first one, first in nobility.
How shall I win to her people? Far in Anéyzateyn
  feed they their flocks in the Spring-time, we in the Gháilem.
Yet it was thou, my beloved, willed we should sunder thus,
  bridled thyself the swift striders, black night encompassing.
Fear in my heart lay a captive, seeing their camel-herds
  herded as waiting a burden, close to the tents of them,
Browsing on berries of khímkhim, forty-two milch-camels,
  black as the underwing feathers set in the raven's wing,
Then was it 'Abla enslaved thee showing her tenderness,
  white teeth with lips for kissing. Sweet was the taste of them,

Sweet as the vial of odours sold by the musk sellers,
    fragrant the white teeth she showed thee, fragrant the
                                  mouth of her.
So is a garden new planted fresh in its greenery,
    watered by soft-falling raindrops, treadless, untenanted.
Lo, on it rain-clouds have lighted, soft showers, no hail in them,
    leaving each furrow a lakelet bright as a silverling.
Pattering, plashing they fell there, rains at the sunsetting,
    wide-spreading runlets of water, streams of fertility,
Mixed with the humming of bees' wings droning the daylight long,
    never a pause in their chaunting, gay drinking-choruses.
Blithe iteration of bees' wings, wings stuck in harmony,
    sharply as steel on the flint-stone, light-handed smithy strokes.
Sweet thou shalt rest till the morning all the night lightly there,
    while I my red horse bestriding ride with the forayers.
Resting-place more than the saddle none have I, none than he
    warhorse of might in the rib-bones – deep is the girth of him.

Say, shall a swift Shadaníeh bear me to her I love
    one under ban for the drinker, weaned for the foal of her,
One with the tail carried archwise, long though the
                              march hath been,
    one with the firm foot atrample, threading the labyrinths?
Lo, how she spurneth the sand-dunes, like to the ear-less one,
    him with the feet set together: round him young ostriches
Troop like the cohorts of Yémen, herded by 'Ajemis,
    she-camel cohorts of Yéman, herded by stammerers.
Watching a beacon they follow, led by the crown of him
    carried aloft as a howdah, howdah where damsels sit,
Him the small-headed, returning, fur-furnished Ethiop,
    black slave, to Thu-el-Ashíra; – there lie his eggs in it.

Lo, how my nága hath drinken deeply in Dóhraydeyn;
    how hath she shrunk back in Déylam, pools of the enemy,
Shrunk from its perilous cisterns, scared by the hunting one,
    great-headed shrieker of evening, clutched to the flank of her.
Still to her offside she shrinketh, deemeth the led-cat there
    Clawing the more that she turneth; – thus is the fear of them.
Lo, she hath knelt in Ridá-a, pleased there and murmuring
    soft as the sweet-fluting rushes crushed by the weight of her.
Thickly as pitch from the boiling oozeth the sweat of her,
    pitch from the cauldron new-lighted, fire at the sides of it,
Oozeth in drops from the ear-roots. Wrathful and bold is she,
    proud in her gait as a stallion hearing the battle-cry.

Though thy fair face concealest still in thy veil from me,
    yet am I he that hath captured horse-riders how many!
Give me the praise of my fair deeds. Lady, thou knowest it,
    kindly am I and forbearing, save when wrong presseth me.
Only when evil assaileth, deal I with bitterness;
    then am I cruel in vengeance, bitter as colocynth.

Sometime in wine was my solace. Good wine, I drank of it,
    suaging the heat of the evening, paying in white money,
Quaffing in goblets of saffron, pale-streaked with ivory,
    hard at my hand their companion, the flask to the left of me.
Truly thus bibbing I squandered half my inheritance;
    yet was my honour a wide word. No man had wounded it.
Since that when sober my dew-fall rained no less generous:
    thou too who knowest my nature, thou too be bountiful!
How many loved of the fair ones have I not buffeted,
    youths overthrown! Ha, the bloodstreams shrill from
                                        the veins of them.

Swift-stroke two-handed I smote him, thrust through the
                                          ribs of him.
   forth flowed the stream of his lifeblood red as anemone.
Ask of the horsemen of Málek, O thou his progeny,
   all they have seen my high deeds. Then shalt thou learn
                                          of them.
   How that I singly among them, clad in war's panoply,
      stout on my warhorse the swift one charged at their chivalry.
Lo, how he rusheth, the fierce one, singly in midst of them,
      waiting anon for the archers closing in front of us.
They that were nearest in battle, they be my proof to thee
      how they have quailed at my war-cry, felt my urbanity.
Many and proud are their heroes, fear-striking warriors,
      men who nor flee nor surrender, yielding not easily.
Yet hath my right arm o'erborne them, thrust them aside from me,
      laid in their proud backs the long spear, – slender the shaft of it.
See, how it splitteth asunder mail-coat and armouring;
      not the most valiant a refuge hath from the point of it.
Slain on the ground have I left him, prey to the lion's brood,
      feast of the wrists and the fingers. Ha, for the sacrifice!

Heavy his mail-cost, its sutures, lo, I divided them
      piercing the joints of the champion; brave was the badge
                                          of him.
Quick-handed he with the arrows, cast in the winter-time,
      raider of wine-seller's signboards, blamed as a prodigal.
He, when he saw me down-riding, making my point at him,
      showed me his white teeth in terror, nay, but not smilingly.
All the day long did we joust it. Then were his finger tips
      stained as though dipped in the íthlem, dyed with
                                          the dragon's blood,

Till with a spear-thrust I pierced him, once and again with it,
  last, with a blade of the Indies, fine steel its tempering,
Smote him, the hero of stature, tall as a tamarisk,
  kinglike, in sandals of dun-hide, noblest of all of them.

Oh, thou, my lamb, the forbidden! prize of competitors,
  why did they bid me not love thee? why art thou veiled
                                                        from me?
Sent I my hand-maiden spy-like: Go thou, I said to her,
  bring me the news of my true love, news in veracity.
Go. And she went, and returning: These in unguardedness
  sit, and thy fair lamb among them, waiting thy archery.
Then was it turned she towards me, fawn-necked in gentleness,
  noble in bearing, gazelle-like, milch-white the lip of it.

Woe for the baseness of 'Amru, lord of ingratitude!
  Verily thanklessness turneth souls from humanity.
Close have I kept to the war-words thy father once spoke to me,
  how I should deal in the death-play, when lips part and
                                                      teeth glitter,
When in the thick of the combat heroes unflinchingly
  cry in men's ears their defiance, danger forgot by them.
Close have I kept them and stood forth their shield from
                                                    the enemy,
  calling on all with my war-cries, circling and challenging.
There where the horsemen rode strongest I rode out in front
                                                        of them,
  hurled forth my war-shout and charged them; – no man
                                              thought blame of me.
Antar! they cried; and their lances, well-cord in slenderness,
  pressed to the breast of my warhorse still as I pressed on them.

Doggedly strove we and rode we. Ha, the brave stallion!
  now is his breast dyed with blood-drops, his star-front
                                    with fear of them!
Swerved he, as pierced by the spear-points. Then in his beautiful
  eyes stood the tears of appealing, words inarticulate.
If he had learned our man's language, then had he called to me:
  if he had known our tongue's secret, then had he cried to me.

Thus to my soul came consoling; grief passed away from it
  hearing the heroes applauding, shouting: Ho, Antar, ho!
Deep through the sand-drifts the horsemen charged with
                                    teeth grimly set,
  urging their war-steeds, the strong-limbed, weight bearers
                                    all of them.
Swift the delúls too I urged them, spurred by my eagerness
  forward to high deeds of daring, deeds of audacity.
Only I feared lest untimely drear death should shorten me
  e'er on the dark sons of Démden vengeance was filled for me.
These are the men that reviled me, struck though I struck
                                    them not,
  vowed me to bloodshed or evil or e'er I troubled them.
Nay, let their hatred o'erbear me! I care not. The sire of them
  slain lies for wild beasts and vultures. Ha! for the sacrifice!

Ántara was of the tribe of Abs, son of the ruling Sheikh Sheddad
and his Abyssinian concubine. He was the model knight errant
who laboured nobly to win the love of his cousin and efface his
illegitimacy and the prejudice against his dark skin. The Muslim
King Arthur who died in AD 615 fighting the Tai tribe.

The Ode of Ibn Kolthúm

Ha! The bow! Fill it high, a fair morning wine-cup!
　　Leave we naught of the lees of Andarína.
Rise, pour forth, be it mixed, let it foam like saffron!
　　tempered thus will we drink it, ay, free-handed.
Him who grieves shall it cure, his despites forgotten;
　　nay, but taste it in tears, it shall console thee.
He, the hoarder of wealth, with the hard face fear-lined,
　　whilst he tasteth, behold him freely giving.
Thou, O mother of Amru, the cup deniest;
　　yet, the right is the wine should pass thy right-hand.
Not the worst of thy three friends is he thou scornest,
　　he for whom thou hast poured no draught of morning.
O the cups that I quaffed in Baálabékki!
　　O the bowls of Damascus, Kaisarína!
Sad fate stands at the door, and uninvited
　　takes us marked for his own at the hour predestined.

Hold, draw rein, ere we sunder, sweet camel-rider;
　　list awhile to my words, nor idly answer.
Wait. Of thee I would know how came the estrangement,
　　whence this haste to betray a friend too faithful?
Tell the fear of that day, what blows! what woundings!
　　what refreshment I poured on thy kin's eyelids!
Each today is foredoomed. And who knows tomorrow,
　　who the after of days, the years we see not?

She her beauty shall show thee, if thou shouldst find her
　　far from injurious eyes, in desert places.

Fair white arms shall she show, as a white she-camel's,
    pure as hers the long-necked one, yet unmounted.
Twin breasts smooth, shalt thou see, as of ivory polished,
    guarded close from the eyes, the hands of lovers.
Waist how supple, how slim! Thou shalt span it sweetly;
    fair flanks sloped to thine eyes and downward bending.
Broad her hips for desire, than thy tent door wider;
    nay, but thine is thy waist, thine own for madness.
Ankles twain, as of marble, are hers. I hear them
    clanking, clattering on, as her anklets rattle.
None have grieved as I grieve, not she, Om Sákbin,
    roaring loud for her lost one, her colt-camel.
None hath grieved as I grieve, not she, the mother
    mourning nine of her sons, her home their red grave.
So recalled I youth's time, and aloud with longing
    wept at the thought of her gone, her howdah fleeting,
Till before me the plain of Yemáma spreading
    flashed, its points in the sun like a foe unsheathing.

O thou Lord Ibn Hind, be thy wrath less quick-breathed;
    wait the word of our mouth, the whole truth spoken,
How each day we ride forth, our banners pure-white,
    how each night we return, our banners red-dyed.
Days of fighting had we, and of joyous glory,
    whilst we smote at the king, his dues denying,
Whilst we vanquished the man their tribes had named king,
    him, the chief they had crowned, their world's-protector.
Stood our horses before him asweat with combat,
    wreathed the reins on their necks, their hind-feet resting.
Near him built we our tents, Dhu-tulúh our outpost,
    El Shamáat at our hand, his riders routed.

Fled the dogs of their tribes from our spear-points howling;
  lo, their thorn we have cut from root to branches.
They who come to our wheat-mill have known our mill-stones;
  they who came for our corn have been stayed for grinding.
Let the mill-cloth be spread in the East lands Nejd-wards;
  be our corn the Kodáat, their tribes assembled.
You as guests to our door in your guile came smiling;
  see, the high feast is served, yourselves the banquet.
Fairly entertained we and plied with victual;
  just at dawn it began, our millstone grinding.
We the tribes have supplied, have upheld their charges,
  borne the burden alone they laid upon us.
Pierced have we with our spear-points their backs the fleers,
  smitten low with our swords and pruned their proud ones.
Lances black of the Khótti are ours, how slender,
  swords that hiss in our hands, to impale and pare them.
Yea, the heads of their mighty have rolled before us,
  loads let loose on a road from beasts unburned.
Still with might we assailed, we pushed, we pressed them,
  lopped their heads at the neck, laid bare their shoulders.
Hate for hate have we given, in deeds revealing
  all the strength of our wrong, our long-pent anger.
Heirs are we of our wrath, as Maád well knoweth;
  glory deal we and wounds, as our right proveth.
When surprise is our lot, and the tent-roofs tumble,
  – sudden raid of the foe – we defend our neighbour.
Bite we sharp with our swords, nor apportion mercy,
  swift ere these shall have seen the hand that smited them.
Reckless we in the melée, our swords with their swords;
  wooden swords you had deemed theirs in hands of children;
Deemed our garments and theirs, their robes and our robes,
  dyed had been in the vats – so red a purple!

Men there were in their fear held back and faltered;
　　terror clutched at their lips, their fate before them.
We alone, like Mount Ráhwa unmoved, in squadrons
　　stood protecting the weak, their battle-winners.
All we held in our youth to be slain for glory,
　　ay, and our gray-beard fighters, our old campaigners,
Doughty challengers we of them, all ill-comers,
　　Girt for crossing of swords, their sons with our sons,
This day going in fear of our children's fair lives,
　　faring forth in a band and as swift dispersing;
That day freed and secure, the alarm forgotten,
　　raiding we in our turn on a far-off foray.
Ours the captain of Júshm, our chief Ibn Béker,
　　Breaker he of the tribes, the weak, the strong tribes.
Not again shall they tell it, the envious nations,
　　how we humbled our heads awhile before them.
Not again shall they fool us or jest against us;
　　lo, the cheek of the proud with pride we out-cheek.

Tell us, Prince Ibn Hind, on what guile thou buildest?
　　how should we to thy kingship yield obedience?
Tell us, 'Amru the King, by what subtle reason
　　dreamest thou to cajole our slandered homage?
Words – nay, threats – thou hast hurled. But O 'Amru, softly!
　　these were well for thy slaves, thy mother's bondsmen.
Think! Our lances, how oft have other foemen
　　failed, before thee, to bend them, to make them pliant.
So the lance-head of iron which bites the lance-shaft,
　　twists to grip of the hand and makes a weapon;
Stiff it grows in the grasp, till aloft it jangles,
　　rives the head of the foe and his who forged it.

Who has dared thee to tell of Júshm Ibn Béker,
    him as wanting in war, our proud forefather?
Are not we too of 'Alkama, heirs in glory,
    his, the fortress of fame? Today we hold it.
Come not we of Muhálhil? Nay, more and better,
    come not we of Zohéyr, of the nobles noblest.
Ours Attáb and Kolthúm, in ascent out fathers;
    we the heirs of their fame, our first possession.
We with Búrati too, as all wot, claim kinship,
    him, the shield of the weak, as we too shield them.
All are ours, and Koléyb, the renowned great fighter.
    Whatso is in the world of fame is our fame.
Who dares link our she-camel with his, lo, straight way
    broken lieth the neck-rope, the neck too broken.
Firm are we in our faith. Thou shalt find none surer,
    no such men of their word to bind and loosen.
We, the day of the beacons on high Kházara,
    gave, and more, of our aid than all the aiders.
We the stronghold of Thú-urát held how stoutly,
    starved our nágas within it on what lean pasture!
We the right wing defended, the day of battle;
    next us fought too the left wing, no less our brethren.
Whoso stood in their path have beheld them charging;
    whoso paused on our way we slew before us.
These returned with the plunder, with wealth made captive,
    we with lords in our train and kings in fetters.
Ho, ye children of Béker, aroint ye, boasters!
    Know ye nought of our name? Must ye learn our glory?
Nay, ye know of our valour, our hands with your hands,
    fights how fierce with the spears, with the arrows singing.
Helmets ours are of steel, stout shields from Yémen,
    tall the swords in our hands and poised for striking.

Mail-coats ours; in the sun you have seen them gleaming;
   hawberks wide for our swords, of a noble wideness.
Ay, and after the fight, you have seen us naked,
   creased the skin of our limbs like leathern jerkins,
Seen the bend of our backs, where the armour pressed us,
   scored with waves, like a pool the South-wind blowing.

Lo, the mares we bestride at the dawn of battle!
   sleek-coat mares, the choice ones; ourselves have
                                                weaned them.
Charge they mail-clad together, how red with battle,
   red the knots of their reins as dyed with blood-stains.
Are not these the inheritance of our fathers?
   shall not we to our sons in turn bequeath them?
We the vanguard in arms. Behind us marching
   trail our beautiful ones, our wives close-guarded.
They it was who imposed on our lives a promise,
   still their badge to uphold from all assaulting,
Ay, and plunder to bring, fair mares and helmets,
   noble prisoners, bound with ropes, to serve them.
Thus go we to the war. And behold, the clansmen
   seized with fear of us fly and form alliance,
While our maidens advance with a proud gait swaying,
   like to drinkers of wine, with spoils o'erladen,
Camel-riders each one, of Júshm Ibn Béker,
   beauty theirs and the blood, and all noble virtues,
Feeders sure of our mares. Yet they tell us lightly:
   none will we for our lovers, save the valiant.
Since the fence of the fair is but this, the sword-stroke,
   this, the shredding of limbs as a plaything shredded.
Thus say they, and we hear them, our swords unsheathing
   yet are all men our sons who kneel before us.

Heads we toss of the proud, as you see a ball tossed,
    kicked in play by the youths that urge the football.
All men know us of old in Maád, the tribesmen,
    when our tents we have built in the open pastures.
Feasters are we of men with the men that love us,
    slayers are we of men, the men that hate us;
Rightful lords of the plain, to forgive and welcome;
    where we will have pitched. Who has dared gainsay us?
Still with ire we deny in the face of anger;
    still with smiles we accede to smiles of pleading.
Faithful aye to the weak who have made submission;
    ruthless aye to the proud who raise rebellion.
Ours the right of the wells, of the springs untroubled;
    theirs the dregs of the plain, the rain-pools trampled.
Nay, but ask of the tribes, Tommáh, Domíyan,
    what the worth of our hands, our hearts in battle.
Nay, but ask of the king, when he came to bend us,
    what of pride we returned to his words of evil.
Lo, the lands we o'errun, till the plains grow narrow,
    lo, the seas will we sack with our war-galleys.
Not a weanling of ours shall win to manhood,
    find the world at his knees, its great ones kneeling.

Sheikh of the Bein Taghleb tribe when aged just fifteen.
He died just twenty-two years before the Islamic era.

The Ode of El Hárith

Lightly she took her leave of me, Asmá-u,
  went no whit as a guest who outstays a welcome;
Went forgetting our trysts, Burkát Shemmá-u,
  all the joys of our love, our love's home, Khalsá-u.
Muhayyátu, she thee forgets, Sifáhu,
  thee, Fitákon, Aádibon, thee Wafá-u.
Thee, Riád el Katá, thee, vale of Shérbub,
  'Anak, thee, Shobatána, and thee, Ablá-u.
Nay, ye lost are to me with my lost glory;
  nay, though tears be my meat, weeping wins no woman.
Yet, a snare to my eyes, afar was kindled
  fire by night on the hill. It was Hind's love-beacon.
Blindly now do I watch her from Khezáza;
  woe, the warmth of it, woe, – thought the hilltops redden!
Woe its blaze from Akík, its flame from Shakhséyn!
  woe the signal alight for me, Hind's love-incense!

Out on tears and despair! I go free, sundered:
  here stand doors of relief. Who hath fled escapeth.
Mount I light on my nága. No hen ostrich
  swift as she, the tall trotter, her brood behind her,
Hearing voices who fled from them, the hunters,
  pressing fast on her way from mid-eve to nightfall.
Nay, behold her, my noble one, upheaving
  motes and dust on her path, as a cloud pursuing.
All un-shoed are the feet of her, her sandals
  strewn how wide on her road by the rough
                                        rocks loosened.
Joy thus I take on her, the summer heat through.
  All but I had despaired, – like a blinded camel.

O the curse of men's eyes, of their ill-speaking!
    Danger deep and a wound did their false lips deal us.
Have not these with their tongues made small things
                                              great things,
    telling lies of our lives, our kind kin, the Arákim?
Mixing blame with un-blame for us, till flouted
    stand we, proven of wrong, with the guilty guiltless.
All, say these, that have run with us the wild ass,
    ours are they, our allies, as our own tribe their tribes.
Thus by night did they argue it and plot it,
    rose at dawn to their treating and stood forth shouting.
Loud the noise of their wrath. This called, that answered;
    great the neighings of steeds and the camel-roarings.

Ho, thou weaver of wild words, thou tale-painter!
    must it thus be for ever and thus with Amru?
Not that slanders are strange. Their words we heed not;
    long ere this have we known them, their lips, the liars.
High above them we live. Hate may not harm us,
    fenced in towers of renown, our unstained bright honour.
Long hath anger assailed us, rage, denial;
    long hath evil prevailed in the eyes of evil.
Nathless, let them assault. As well may Fortune
    hurl its spears at the rocks, at the cloud-robed mountains.
Frowneth wide of it Fear. Fate shall not shake it.
    Time's worst hand of distress shall disturb it never.

O thou king Iramíyan! with thee circle
    riders keen of their steel to cut off thy foeman.
King art thou, the all-just, of Earth's high-walkers
    foremost, first in the world, its all-praise surpassing.

If of wrong there be aught untamed, unstraightened,
  being but word to our chiefs; they should deal out justice.
Set thy gaze on the hills, on Mílha, Sákib.
  See the slain unavenged, while alive their slayers.
Probe the wound of our anger, though thou hurt us,
  yet shall truth be approved and the falsehood flouted.
Else be thou of us silent, and we silent,
  closing lids on our wrong, though the mote lies under.
Yet, refusing the peace, whomso you question,
  he shall speak in our praise, shall assign us worship.

O the days of the war, of our free fighting,
  raidings made in surprise, the retreats, the shoutings!
How our nágas we scourged from Sâf el Bahrain,
  pressing hard to the end, to our goal El Hása!
Turned had we on Temím before Monárrem,
  taken their daughters for wives, their maids
                                    for handmaids.
None might stay us nor strive us. The stoutest
  though turning availed not nor their feet flying,
Nay, nor mountain might hide nor plain protect them;
  blackness burnt in the sun, it might bring no succour.
Thou, O King, art the master. Where in all lands
  standeth one of thy height? There is none beside thee.

Lo, how stiff was our stand for him, El Móndir.
  Say, were we, as were these, Ibn Hind's base herdsmen?
Let the Tághlebi slain in their blood answer,
  unavenged where they lie. In the dust we spilled it.
He, the king, when in that high place Maisúna's
  tent he built, for her who so loved Ausá-u,

What of turbulent folk did he there gather,
  broken men of the tribes, ragged, hungry vultures!
Dates and water to all he gave in bounty.
  God's revenge on the guilty they called his soldiers.
You the weight of them proved with your mad challenge,
  brought them blind on your back by your idle boasting.
Nay, they gave you no false words, laid no ambush;
  broad before you at noon you beheld them marching.

Ho, thou bearer of tales to Amru, babbler!
  when of this shall the end be, how soon the silence?
Proofs he hath at our hands, three honest tokens,
  each enough for his eyes of our faith unswerving.
First when came from Shakík at him the warlords,
  all Máad in their tribes, with each clan a banner.
Mail-clad men were there their chieftain Káis,
  he, the prince Karahíyan, a rock, a stronghold.
With him sons of the brave, of freeborn ladies;
  naught might stand to their shock save alone our
                                        sword-blades.
Them we drove back with wounds like the out-rushing
  streams with goatskins are pricked; it was thus their
                                        blood flowed;
Drove them back to Thahlána its strong places,
  scattered, drenched in their gore where the thigh
                                        wounds spouted.
Struck we stern at the lives of them; then trembled
  deep our spears in their well, like a long-roped bucket.
Only God shall appraise how we misused them;
  none hath claimed for their lives the uncounted blood price.
Next with Hójra it was, Ibn im Katáma;
  with him rode the Iráni, – how red their armour!

Roused, a lion, he chargeth, his feet thudding,
    yet as Spring to the poor in the day of their hunger.
Chains we struck from the hands of Imr el Káis;
    long the days of his grief were, his months of bondage.
We, when Jaun of Aál Beni 'Aus sought us,
    rock-strong with him a band of unyielding horsemen,
Nothing feared, though the dust of them around us
    swept the plain like a smoke by the war-flame kindled.
Put we swords on his neck, Ghássan, for Móndir,
    wrath that less than our right was the blood price counted.
Lastly brought we the nine of the royal blood,
    all their wealth in our hands, an unnumbered booty.
Amr was a son of ours Ibn Om Eyyási;
    close in kinship he came, when he gave the dowry.
Let this stand to our count, our power in pleading!
    land with land are we knit, by the strong
                            ones strengthened.
Hold the tongue of your boasting, your vain glory,
    else be yourselves the blind, on yourselves ill-fortune.

O, remember the oath of Thil Majázi,
    all that was of old time, the fair words, the pledges.
Flee the evil, the hate! Shall men gainsay it,
    that which stands on the skin, for the whim of any?
Think how we with yourselves the fair deed signed there,
    did the thing we should do, and no less, our duty.
Faction all and injustice! As well, when feasting,
    take, for vow of a sheep, a gazelle in payment!
Was it ours, say, the blame of it all, when Kíndah
    took your booths for a spoil, that of us you claim it?
Was it ours that foul deed of him, Eyádi?
    are we bound with his rope, like a loaded camel?

Not by us were these done to their death, nor Káis,
      nay, nor Jéndal by us, nor he Haddá-u.
Theirs, not ours, were the cry of Beni Atíkeh;
      clean of blame are our hands since you tore the treaties.
Eighty went of Temím, – in their right hands lances;
      each a sentence of death, when they went against you,
Left your sons where they lay sword-slashed and
                                                                              bloodstained,
      brought a tumult of spoil till men's ears were deafened.
Is it ours the ill-deed of the man Hanífa?
      ours the strife of all time, Earth's arrears of evils?
Ours the wrong of Kodáat? Nay, 'tis all injustice;
      not for these and their sins are our hands indicted.
Not for these, nor their raid on the Béni Rázah;
      who shall approve their claim in Nitá, in Búrka?
Long they cringed for a spoil, these camel-cravers,
      yet not one did we give, not a black nor white one;
Left them bare till they fled with their backs broken,
      all unwatered their thirst, unassuaged their vengeance;
Horsemen hard on their tracks, El Fellak's riders,
      pity none in their hand, in their heart no sparing.
Ours it was, the dominion of all these peoples,
      ours till El Móndir ruled, the sweet rain of heaven.

Thou, O King, art the master. Thou our witness
      stoodst the day of Hayáreyn. Our proof is proven!

El Hárith ibn Hiliza was of the Beni Bekr tribe. His ode
was recited to King Amr ibn Hind, judging a feud with
the Beni Taghleb tribe in AD 560.

Index of first lines

Index of poem titles